BEYOND
KNIT
&
PURL

Beyond Knit & Purl

TAKE YOUR KNITTING
TO THE NEXT LEVEL

Kate Atherley

COOPERATIVE PRESS
Cleveland, Ohio

ISBN 13: 978-1-937513-03-0
Second Edition (v2.1)
Published by Cooperative Press
www.cooperativepress.com

Text © 2011, Kate Atherley
Model Photos © 2011, Kristen Caldwell
with the exception of aran sweater photos page 86, Adrian Bizilia and additional photos by Lise
Beauchesne and Shannon Okey.
Author headshot page 127 by Natalie Selles.
Models: Jenny Barnett Rohrs, Kate Atherley, Arabella Proffer, Rowan Garcia
Instructional photos © 2011, Caro Sheridan
Illustration page 104, © 2011, MJ Kim

Knitting symbols courtesy of Aire River Design (home.earthlink.net/~ardesign/index.htm).
Charts made with Knit Visualizer (knitfoundry.com).

COOPERATIVE PRESS
Senior Editor: Shannon Okey
Technical Editor: Stephannie Tallent
with additional technical editing by Alexandra Virgiel
Copyediting: Heather Ordover

For Hilda, who got me started, and for Norman, who keeps me going.

TABLE OF CONTENTS

Introduction

I've been teaching knitting for nearly 10 years, and this book is a direct result of my experiences as a teacher.

The craft has experienced a renaissance over the past decade. As a long-standing knitter, I'm thrilled to see all these new knitters joining the fold.

Every week students ask me the same questions: *What's easy to knit? What's a good first project? Where can I find good patterns?* And inevitably: *I'm tired of scarves. What's next?* This book is my answer to all those students, to help them find their way once they know how to knit and purl.

All new knitters have run headlong into the same challenge that I did when I first started knitting: there's a big gulf between knowing how to knit and purl and knowing how to choose and successfully work a pattern.

The first section of this book is designed to address that particular gap. We'll consider how to choose and assess the difficulty level of pattern, and explore the types of projects that are good for newer knitters. And I'll show you how to successfully work your pattern—how to choose which size to make, what this gauge business is all about, and how to actually read it. *Beyond Knit & Purl* is designed to be both an instructional manual and a reference.

The second section of the book tackles key knitting techniques that allow you to broaden your skills and move beyond scarves: shaping, working in the round, socks, cables, lace and colorwork. Each chapter in the second section starts with a "how to" guide to get you started and a mini-project to allow you to practice your new skills. These mini projects are designed to take no more than an evening or two and are a great "sandbox" to try a few things out. And if you like what you're doing, there are three more projects using these techniques, each building your skills further.

Along the way, you'll find plenty of tips and knitterly advice in boxes like this …

> ## KNITTERLY ADVICE
>
> *Remember to savor your knitting: the process is at least as important and fun as the product. Take time, enjoy and have fun.*
>
> *— Mary-Cate Garden, knitter*

… as well as Dirty Secrets that will help you, too. These tip boxes are designed to add to the information presented or give you a quick point of reference. It's like having a good knitting teacher or stitching group at your side!

Chapter 1: Choosing a Pattern

You can knit—and now you're ready to start your first project from a pattern. It might be your first large project, such as a sweater, or your first go at branching out beyond scarves. No matter your knitting experience, a few simple rules can help you choose a pattern that's appropriate to your skill level—and to your needs.

After all, the right pattern choice isn't just about what skills you have, it's also about what sort of project you want. Sometimes, you're looking for something to engage and challenge you; sometimes you want a project that's easy and fun.

I always have a couple of things on the go—something easy that doesn't require too much attention, and something a bit "meatier." The easy projects are great for knitting in the car or on the bus or train—or when you want to really pay attention to what's on TV; more challenging projects are best for when your partner is watching something you're not really interested in, for long plane rides, or even quiet Sunday afternoons listening to music.

It's also nice to have a second, easier project at hand when I get stuck or frustrated with a more challenging project. Sometimes I want to knit but I don't have much time or I'm simply too tired for a challenge.

So what's easy and restful, and what's challenging?

EASY OR EXPERIENCED?

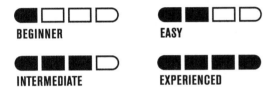

The Craft Yarn Council is also responsible for these symbols, which you will see on some patterns. Unfortunately, one designer's Easy is another designer's Intermediate...and so on. We'll discuss best practices for determining whether a pattern is right for you in the next chapter.

A fair number of publishers do provide indicators of difficulty level. Knitty.com, for example, has a rating system ranging from Mellow to Extraspicy. The Craft Yarn Council of America has established a rating system—Easy, Intermediate, and Experienced—which many US publications use.

Typically, a beginner level pattern will focus on straightforward stitch patterns—garter and stockinette stitch—and will have minimal shaping, that is, not too much in the way of increasing or decreasing. An easy project will have a bit more going on in the way of increasing and decreasing and add other pattern stitches like ribbing or seed stitch. These projects might also have a seam or two, or some stripes.

Intermediate projects will add pattern stitches like cables, lace or colorwork; or they might be worked in the round. There will be more to track in terms of shaping and more finishing work—seams, also possibly special bind offs or edgings.

As to experienced patterns—often, these patterns will explain what's challenging about them. Typically, you'll see interesting shapings, multiple pieces that have to be sewn up, and multiple pattern stitches worked at the same time.

If you're just starting out with patterns, it's a good idea to find one that has an indicator of the difficulty level and gives a bit of explanation of what sorts of techniques are used. Publishers such as Patons, Red Heart, Bernat, and Lion Brand always provide a difficulty level, as do most magazines.

I LEARNED TO KNIT LAST WEEK – AM I READY FOR SOCKS?

In general, these guidelines can help you to figure out what's easier and what's more challenging. Consider the basic shape, the style of the garment, and the pattern stitch used, and refer to the charts on pages 14–15.

If you want to try garments, I highly recommend starting with babies' or kid's things. They don't take long to knit, don't use up much yarn, and are a nice "sandbox" to try out some new things. If there are no small people in your life, charities will often taken donations of knitted goods. Babies' and kids' items are gratefully received at many women's shelters, for example. A baby isn't going to worry if the project doesn't look perfect; the adorableness of a baby does an excellent job of overshadowing any possible mistakes in the sweater he or she is wearing. Nor will a baby mind if you found the yarn in the bargain bin.

Check out free patterns on Knitty or yarn company websites for baby's wear. A list of good websites offering free patterns is on page 37. And remember, there's nothing to say you shouldn't take on a more challenging project—something a little beyond your level or experience. It's a great way to stretch your skills—just expect that you'll really need to pay attention as you work and you might need to do some research to learn required skills. I've seen knitters who have very successfully taken on socks and lace immediately after finishing their first scarves.

ONE PAGE OR TWELVE?

Beyond these simple guidelines, taking a good look at the pattern itself can provide many clues to the level of difficulty.

Look at how many pieces there are in the project: is there a schematic with multiple pieces like this one?

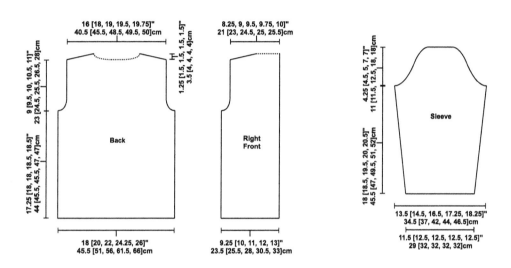

Look for and count section headings: For example, *Back, Front, Sleeve*—fewer pieces makes for an easier knit.

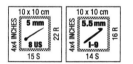 **Look at the gauge and needle size listed in the pattern**. (In the UK and Canada, the word "tension" is often used). The image at left is often used on yarn ball bands to indicate the recommended gauge and suggested needle sizes for that yarn. Compare the two if you would like to substitute yarns. (See Chapter 2 for information about buying yarn and making substitutions). Note that there are two different sets of numbers here: one for knitting (left) and one for crochet (right)—don't confuse the two.

Larger needles and fewer stitches in 4 inches/10cm means thicker yarn, which means the project will be quicker, and the yarn easier to manage. 10–16 stitches in four inches using 6mm–10mm or even larger needles is easier and quicker than 30 stitches in four inches using 2.5mm needles. (More details on gauge are available on page 19).

However, some knitters find extra-large needles challenging to work with—for example, children or those with smaller hands may have more trouble manipulating a larger needle than a smaller one—with time you may also find you prefer projects that are worked within a certain range of needle sizes. Anything worked with a needle between 5mm (US #8) and 8 mm (US #11) will be easy to handle and relatively fast.

Read through the finishing instructions: Fewer special finishing instructions usually means an easier project.

Look at the length of the pattern: If it's got 12 pages, chances are it's going to be more challenging. But a half-page pattern may not be all that easy. If it's *crazy* short, scan through it to make sure all the required info is there. Does it have yarn and needle info? Gauge? And do the actual instructions make sense to you? Read through them. You're not necessarily going to be able to figure everything out on the spot, but you'll be able to get a sense of whether you feel confident about it.

A pattern that spells out every row ...

> Row 1 [RS]: *K2, p2; repeat from * to end.
> Row 2 [WS]: As per Row 1.
> Repeat the last 2 rows until piece measures 4 inches.

... is going to be easier to follow that one that doesn't (e.g. "Work 4 inches in k2 p2 ribbing"). The second example isn't wrong—but it does require a bit more knowledge to work.

Trust your instincts—some patterns are easier to read than others. If you can't make sense of a pattern, look for something else.

SIGNS THAT A PATTERN IS GOING TO BE CHALLENGING

- Multiple pieces: a back, two fronts, a collar stand, two edgings, a belt, and half a page of finishing instructions.
- Teeny tiny yarn and needles: anything that calls for more than 30 sts in 4 inches, or anything smaller than 2.25mm (US #1) needles.
- Long paragraphs of instructions that are hard to read.
- The words "at the same time": this means that there are multiple shapings or other details you'll need to track.
- The words "keeping pattern correct" or its more formal version "keeping continuity of pattern": this means that you'll need to figure out how to work increases and decreases into some kind of pattern stitch.
- The words "reversing shapings": this most often means that the pattern has been edited down for space and will require you to do some thinking.

A RELIABLE SOURCE

The internet is an amazing source of knitterly guidance and goodies. There are thousands of free patterns available online. Not every pattern is of equal quality, however. The level of challenge in working a pattern isn't just about the knitting techniques, but also about how it's written.

Just because a knitter comes up with a great design doesn't mean that she has written up the pattern well—designing and pattern writing are two entirely different skills. There might be typos, missing information, or perhaps vague or misleading instructions. I've had a student buy a pattern online only to discover that it was missing information about the yarn and the needles used, making it almost impossible to actually knit.

One publisher of very popular free patterns is based in a non-English-speaking country. They provide translations of their patterns that are usually fairly good, but oddities can sometimes creep in. I recently encountered an instruction to "leave stitches standing," and it took me a few minutes to realize that the pattern wanted me to slip the stitches to a holder.

Therefore, if you're browsing for a free pattern, it's best to keep to reliable sources. Digital publishers and websites such as Knitty.com employ technical editors to review the patterns and make sure that they not only work, but that they are clearly written. Yarn companies often provide free patterns, and not only can you feel comfortable that the patterns have been proofread, but in most cases, they also provide an email address to allow you to ask questions if you do run into a problem.

KNITTERLY ADVICE

When someone asks you to knit 'one of those' for them, offer to teach them how to do it themselves, with a smile, and mean it.

— Amy R. Singer, knitty.com

That's not to say using a self-published pattern—whether sold through Ravelry or published on a blog—is necessarily a bad idea. In many cases, designers do have their patterns proofread and test knitted. The best way to determine if a self-published pattern is a safe bet is to look it up on Ravelry. You can see how many knitters have worked the project and check if there are notes or updates to the pattern. If lots of knitters have successfully made it, chances are it's a good pattern. There's even a difficulty rating provided by Ravelry, which is set by knitters who have worked the project.

If it's published on a blog, see if there are comments on the blog posting from knitters who have worked with the pattern.

MISTAKES DO HAPPEN

Even if it's not a self-published pattern, it's a good idea to check for updates and corrections before you start knitting. No matter how well a pattern is proofread, mistakes can creep in. One recently-published book suffered a small and silly typesetting error—changing a division symbol (÷) to a subtraction symbol (–)—that affected the pattern significantly.

Websites such as Knitty can update patterns in real-time, so if a mistake is found, it's corrected.

The vast majority of print publishers maintain errata listings online, with corrections or updates for issues that have been found. So before you start knitting, look up the pattern online. Go directly to the online source of the pattern and make sure you print the most recent version; if it's a book, Google its title plus the publisher's name with the word "errata."

Once you've chosen the pattern, and made sure you've got the most recent version and any relevant updates, you're ready for the next step.

QUICK TIP

Ravelry.com

www.ravelry.com is a social network for crafters. It's predominantly knitting-focused, but there's a strong crochet presence, too. Crafters create profiles, listing projects they are working on, posting photographs and details of their work and experiences, and participating in discussion forums on a huge range of topics—some entirely social, others are in-depth discussions on techniques and technical aspects of the craft.

It's become an amazing resource for information about people, patterns and yarn. Before you start any project, I recommend you research the pattern and the yarn on Ravelry. You can learn about whether a pattern is easy or more challenging to knit. You can find out how a particular yarn holds up to repeated washing, for example. By looking at pictures of a sweater worn by knitters of different body types, you can see how a particular design might fit you.

Designers make patterns available for download—sometimes free, sometimes for sale—through the Ravelry store functionality. The same advice applies to patterns found on Ravelry as anywhere else, though: research it first. There is no requirement to have a pattern proofread or edited to make it available on Ravelry, so knitters' comments will guide you as to whether it's a good choice or not.

KATE'S TIPS FOR CHOOSING APPROPRIATE PATTERNS

STITCH PATTERNS	SKILLS REQUIRED	DIFFICULTY LEVEL
Garter stitch	Knit.	Beginner.
Stockinette stitch	Knit & purl.	Beginner.
Ribbing	Knit & purl.	Beginner.
Other knit & purl combos – seed stitch, basketweave patterns	Knit & purl; keeping track of pattern rows and stitches.	Easy - requires a bit more attention.
Cables	Working with a cable needle; reading the pattern, reading charts.	Easy if one cable; Intermediate if more than one.
Lace	Increasing and decreasing; counting and keeping track of stitches and pattern rows. Reading the pattern, reading charts.	Intermediate to Advanced.
Stripes	Knit & purl.	Beginner.
Other colorwork	Reading charts.	Intermediate to Advanced.
Entrelac	Increasing, decreasing, picking up stitches.	Intermediate.

SUCCESSFULLY KNITTED?	A GOOD NEXT STEP
A plain scarf or dishcloth	Scarves with pattern stitches like ribbing or other knit & purl combos; dishcloths in pattern stitches, hats (worked flat).
A hat (worked flat)	Cables; hats in the round.
A hat in the round	Wrist warmers, mittens; kid's garments.
Mittens	Socks, toys.
Socks	Gloves; entrelac, garments.
Kids' garments	Adult garments - try a vest first; toys.
Plain, single colors	Stripes.
Stripes	Fair Isle.
Fair Isle	Intarsia.
Cables & socks	Lace.

ITEM	SKILLS REQUIRED	DIFFICULTY LEVEL
Rectangular scarves, shawls, and wraps	Only whatever is required for the pattern stitch (this is generally applicable for all patterns).	Beginner.
Hats	Working in the round, or seaming if it's worked flat.	Easy.
Wrist warmers	Working in the round, or seaming if it's worked flat.	Easy.
Mittens	Working in the round; increasing and decreasing.	Intermediate, but make an excellent skill-builder project.
Gloves	Working in the round; increasing and decreasing; working with small needles and fine yarn; keeping track of pattern rows; working with small pieces.	Intermediate to advanced. Fiddly.
Socks	Working in the round; increasing and decreasing; working with small needles and fine yarn; keeping track of pattern rows.	Intermediate, but easier if worked with thicker yarn and needles.
Toys – teddy bears, etc.	Increasing, decreasing; seaming; keeping track of pattern rows.	Intermediate, but because there's not a lot of knitting can be a good skill-builder project.
Blanket – one piece	Working with a larger number of stitches; keeping track of a pattern.	Beginner to intermediate – can be more challenging simply because of the size of the project; can get boring.
Blanket – in pieces	Seaming.	Beginner to intermediate – can be more interesting if it's got different pieces.
Triangular shawls and wraps	Increasing and decreasing.	Easy if plain; Intermediate if uses pattern stitches.
Pullover vest/sweater	Working in the round or seaming; picking up stitches.	Easy if plain; Intermediate if uses pattern stitches.
Cardigan vest/sweater	Seaming, picking up stitches.	Intermediate.

Chapter 2: Prepping for Success

THE SIZE

As a knitting teacher and yarn store employee, the single biggest problem area for knitters starting a new project is identifying which pattern size to knit. At lot of knitters shy away entirely from sized patterns for this reason alone—they'll tackle the most complex lace, but wouldn't even dream of trying to figure out how to choose a sweater pattern that fits.

It's not nearly as mysterious as it seems. The first thing to do is ignore the sizing information. (Yes, you read that correctly!) That is, ignore any indication of *small, medium, large* and *extra large*. Those are there as just guidelines, nothing more.

Most patterns will list two sets of sizing information—"to fit" and "actual." The indicator "to fit" (or sometimes just "size") is the size of person the designer intends to fit; "actual" is the corresponding garment size. The difference between the two is known as "ease". If a pattern suggests that a garment to fit a 36 inch bust measurement should be 38 inches around, you know it's supposed to be worn fairly close-fitting. If a pattern suggests that a size *small* for a woman's garment should be a 44 inch finished bust measurement, then you know that it's meant to be worn very loose. A garment with zero or "negative ease" is designed to be worn *very* fitted—tights and swimsuits are garments with negative ease, they stretch to fit.

The best way to figure out what size to knit is to find a garment that's similar to the one you want to knit, a garment with a fit that you like, and measure it. More ease makes for a more relaxed fit, less ease makes for a tighter garment; a garment in a heavier yarn needs more ease than a garment worked in sock yarn. Do take into account the designer's guidelines on ease—if the designer is suggesting a 40-inch finished bust measurement for a 36-inch bust size, then the garment is designed to be worn loose and relaxed, and is constructed with that in mind. A garment designed to be worn loose won't have the same shaping or tailoring around the shoulders and armhole as a garment designed to be worn more fitted. A 40 inch garment designed to be worn loose will look pretty terrible on a wearer with a 39 inch bust measurement; it just won't fit right.

When a pattern says a sweater is size *small*, it just means that it's intended to be worn by someone with a smallish stature, that's all. Let the finished measurements of the garment be your guide. For example, I find that for a thinner garment that's worn under a jacket, I like about an inch of ease; for a medium-weight cardigan I like about 2–3 inches of ease; for a heavier fitted pullover I like about 2 inches of ease. For jackets and heavy cardigans, I like 4–5 inches of ease.

Most schematics will look like this.

Many patterns will provide a schematic with measurements, too. They show you both visually and using numbers what is being measured and where, as in the schematic at right. The measurements shown in the schematic are the finished measurements of the piece.

Whether working from a table or schematic, look at the finished bust size and the finished length—and choose which size to knit based on that. If there's no finished sizing information, as with many vintage patterns, you will probably be better off avoiding it. Sizing in this case

STYLE	TYPICAL EASE FOR ADULT GARMENTS
Fitted t-shirt, tank top	*Up to 1 inch*
Fitted sweater	*Up to 1 inch*
Tailored pullover, cardigan	*Up to 2 inches*
Relaxed pullover, cardigan	*2-3 inches*
Outerwear (to be worn with layers underneath)	*4-6 inches*
Oversized jacket or coat	*6 or more inches*

can be especially tricky because fit standards have been very different at different times.

The rules are different for kids' garments—you need less ease on smaller garments—but in general kids' garments are made a little larger and worn oversized to accommodate growth.

THE YARN

A pattern will always specify a yarn (and if it doesn't, again, it's probably a good idea to find another pattern). If you can find that precise yarn, terrific. You can't always, however, and you will need to figure out a good substitute. Consider the following factors when making a yarn substitution: the texture, the coloring, the fiber content and the care instructions—and most importantly, the gauge.

On texture, coloring and fiber content—let the pattern and the photograph of the sample be your guide.

If the pattern has fancy stitch patterns and textural stitches, a smoother yarn is going to be much better to show off the stitchwork. Here, the same pattern has been knit into two swatches, but using different yarns. The cable pattern is barely visible in the fuzzy yarn at right!

And if there's fancy texture and stitchwork, choose a colorway that will show it off. A heavily variegated yarn with strong color changes looks best in plain knitting—it would obscure any patterning you might do. If it's plain knitting, consider a variegated yarn to add visual interest: See the middle photo on this page for an example of plain color showing off a lace texture better than a variegated yarn.

Take the designer's lead: if the designer has used a textured, multicolored yarn, then look for something similar. If the designer has used a solid colored smooth yarn, stay close to that.

And last but not least, consider the care: will the finished object need to be washed often? If so, choose a washable yarn like cotton or superwash wool. If the finished object is going to be gifted to someone who tends to throw things in the washer and dryer, or doesn't have time to handwash—for example, my nephew at college—choose a washable yarn. Pay attention to the washing instructions on the ball band: if a yarn says it's handwash only—it means it.

An example of what can happen to yarn when it's not meant to go in the machine and does! Both swatches were the same size before the one at right was washed.

ON FIBER SUBSTITUTION

Again, take the designer's lead. Different fibers behave differently: for example, wool has natural elasticity, and makes for excellent socks that hold their fit through the day and sweaters that hold their shape over their lifetime; cotton tends to stretch and not bounce back—it's better for items that aren't very fitted, or where shape doesn't matter as much. Alpaca is a heavy fiber that drapes beautifully in lighter pieces, but can sag in larger pieces like jackets. Use the guidelines in the table below to help you.

ITCHINESS VS. SOFTNESS

This swatch is starting to pill from rough treatment

On the itch factor: some people have genuine allergies to animal fibers, some people just find them scratchy and unpleasant to wear. Animal fibers are absolutely my favorite thing to knit, but if the item is being gifted to someone who doesn't like or can't wear wool, I will choose another fiber.

To test for a fiber sensitivity, tie a small length of the yarn to your bra strap and let it dangle under your arm. (For men, tie a length around your neck like a lariat.) Leave it for an hour or so. If a rash or welt appears, remove it and consider allergy testing; if it's just itchy, consider a softer yarn from the same fiber, a blend, or another fiber. And just because one animal fiber doesn't suit you it doesn't mean they will all be a problem. I find alpaca itchy (sadly), but have no problems with sheeps' wool or other animal fibers.

Remember, however, that the softer the yarn, the more likely it is to pill. Friction against the surface of the knitting will cause small balls of fuzz to form. Think about whether the garment will undergo a lot of friction. A hat won't pill so much—a sweater is likely to pill more under the arms where the sleeves rub the body.

HOW MUCH TO BUY

FIBER	PROPERTIES	BEST APPLICATIONS	AVOID
Wool	Excellent insulator—very warm; natural elasticity—bounces back if stretched out.	Anything! Garments, hats, socks, mittens, blankets, ...	Consider the itch factor. Consider superwash vs. not—does it need to be hand-washed, and will that be convenient?
Cotton	Holds color well, washable, ages well.	Washable items, kids' items, baby blankets. Great for lighter socks when blended with wool.	Items where warmth is needed like mittens.
Acrylic, other synthetics	Washable, colorfast, inexpensive.	Best when blended with another fiber like wool or cotton.	Mittens, socks - holds moisture and stays wet and smelly.
Alpaca, llama, vicuna	Very warm, heavy; may be sheddy and pilly. (See comments about softness.)	Smaller pieces and fitted garments, terrific in blends with wool; luxurious accessories.	Big garments - will sag.
Cashmere	Very warm and light; expensive.	Luxury garments, small pieces that go directly next to your skin like cowls, small scarves, hats for bald men. Nice in blends.	Buying enough for a whole garment unless you've won the lottery.
Mohair	Very warm and light; takes dye well. Many find it itchy.	Overgarments like jackets.	Not for garments that will be close to the skin.
Silk	Insulating. Soft and drapey, doesn't pill.	100% silk: Luxury garments, small pieces that go directly next to your skin. Blends: adds sheen and elasticity and warmth to fibres like cotton.	Not good when structured or firm fabrics are needed—e.g. wouldn't be good for bags.

A pattern will call for a specific number of balls/skeins for each size. If you're knitting with the yarn called for, it's a good idea to buy an extra one as insurance. Most good yarn stores will allow you to exchange unused balls or skeins (check your receipt or ask at the time of purchase, just in case).

If you're going to be using another yarn, you need to calculate the yardage required. You can't just do it by number of balls because different yarns might not have the same number of yards in a given ball—indeed, the balls might not even be the same size.

For example, a recently-published pattern called for this yarn:

Berroco Remix [30% Nylon, 27% Cotton, 24% Acrylic, 10% Silk, 9% Linen; 216yd/198m per 100g skein]; color: #3924 Clementine; 6[6, 7, 8, 9, 10, 11] skeins

Classic Elite Solstice is an excellent substitute for this yarn, but how much do you need to buy? If I'm making the largest size, and I bought only 11 balls, I'd be in serious trouble.

Each 50g ball of Classic Elite Solstice has 100 yds; a skein of Remix has 216 yds. The largest size needs 11 skeins: 11 x 216 yds, which is 2376 yds of yarn. 2376 yds ÷ 100 yds is 23.76, meaning you'd need 24 balls of Classic Elite. I'd buy 25 just to be on the safe side. It's all about distance, not number of balls. (If it seems like a lot of the Classic Elite, remember that the 50g balls are significantly less expensive than a 100g skein of the other yarn.)

GAUGE

A pattern will list a gauge. (Or at least it should. If this information is missing from the pattern, it's probably a sign that it's not a well-written pattern and you should maybe find another one.) The gauge indicator is a number of stitches and rows (or rounds) over a certain distance. It's most often measured over 4 inches, e.g. "20 sts and 28 rows = 4 x 4 inches in stockinette stitch using 4.5mm needles". Or you might see it in graphic form, as in the diagram at the left.

It's all about size. If the pattern is to make a hat that is precisely 20 inches around, then to make sure that your finished hat is that size, you need to make sure that your stitches are the right size. That is, your stitches should be the same size as the ones in the designer's sample. And gauge is the way to describe and check that.

It's really about two things: making sure you use an appropriate yarn, and that you're using the right needle size.

No matter how it's shown, the basic information is the same: a number of stitches and rows (or rounds) over a set size square, and a suggested needle size. To check the size of your stitches, you can't just measure a single stitch—they are too small. So we measure a set distance and count the stitches in that distance. It's most usual to use 4 inches (or 10cm) so you can get a decent number to count. (Knitters use 4 inches and 10cm interchangeably — it's like baking, pick a measurement system and go with it. If you're working in inches, stick with it throughout the entire pattern.)

From the gauge indicator, you get information about the size of yarn required. It tells you how many stitches you need to fill up a space 10cm (4 inches) wide, and how many rows/rounds you need to fill up a space 10cm (4 inches) high. A smaller number of stitches means a thicker yarn; a larger number of stitches means a thinner yarn — e.g. 9 sts and 12 rows using 8mm needles is a much thicker yarn than 30 sts and 40 rows using 2.5mm needles.

Patterns sometimes use terms to describe the weight of a yarn—double knitting, worsted, bulky, laceweight. These are rough categories of yarn thicknesses. Choosing a yarn by category only isn't necessarily going to guarantee you match gauge, but shopping by category definitely gets you into the correct section of the yarn store. Within any given category, there is still some variation.

In the last few years, there's been an effort on the part of US companies to establish a numbering system to categorize yarn. They are also ranges, and roughly correspond to the common names. These are the symbols typically used on yarn ball bands and in patterns:

NAME	INTERNATIONAL STANDARD #	GAUGE (IN STOCKINETTE OVER 4 INCHES / 10 CM)	TYPICAL NEEDLE SIZE	TYPICAL USES
Thread		Varies based on needle size used	Depends on the use; usually 2 to 4 mm	Lace
Cobweb	0: Lace			
Lace	0: Lace			
Light fingering	0: Lace	32 sts	2.25 - 2.5 mm	Socks
Fingering	1: Super fine	28 sts	2.5 - 3 mm	Socks, baby garments, accessories
Sport/baby	2: Fine	24-26 sts	3.25 - 3.75 mm	Baby garments, accessories
DK	3: Light	22 sts	4 mm	Garments
Worsted	4: Medium	20 sts	4.5 mm	Garments, afghans
Aran	4: Medium	18 sts	4 - 5 mm	Adult garments, afghans
Bulky/ Chunky	5: Bulky	14-15 sts	6 - 8 mm	Adult garments, accessories
Super Bulky	6: Super Bulky	8-12 sts	8 - 10 mm	Accessories

"Worsted" in particular is a difficult word—for two reasons. The term Aran is used in the UK and Canada, but isn't used in the US, and therefore category 4 becomes very broad. The term worsted is also used to define a particular method for spinning yarn. You often see vintage yarns of all sorts of thicknesses labelled as "knitting worsted".

In older pattern books, especially those originating from the UK, Australia and New Zealand, you might also see "ply" used as a way to describe yarn thickness. Again, this gets confused with the use of the word "ply" to describe how many strands are spun together to make the yarn. The larger the number –e.g. 12-ply—the thicker the yarn is. The name or designation of the yarn is only a guideline after all. If you're not sure what the name of the yarn means, let the gauge indicator be your guide.

No matter what category your yarn falls into, you'll still need to swatch for gauge.

HOW TO CHECK GAUGE

The needle size given in a pattern is strictly a suggestion. It's the needles that the designer used to get that gauge. Each knitter knits differently—some tighter, some looser. My gauge changes seasonally—in the summer, when my hands are warm, I tend to knit looser. Use whatever needle size you need to get that gauge with that yarn. The pattern might call for the same size needles called for on the ball band, it might not. It doesn't matter—start with the ones suggested in the pattern and check until you find the size that works for you.

It can be most tricky if you're using a vintage pattern—if you don't know where it was published, the instruction "Number 3 needles" isn't very helpful. In this case, it's best to look at the gauge and see if you can identify what types of yarns typically knit to that gauge, and then what size needles are used for that yarn. (Or just pick a newer pattern!)

How to check? Knit a swatch using the guidelines in the green box at right and then wash the swatch according to the washing instructions on the ball band.

WHY CAST ON SO MANY?

Some books recommend you just cast on the stated number of stitches and work the stated number of rows—but that's not entirely accurate. No matter how skilled a knitter you are, your edge stitches are always a bit wonky—they are formed differently. So you can't include those in the count. And you can't include the first and last rows, as they get smushed up together with the cast on and bind off. To get an accurate count, you need more stitches and more rows so you can measure in the middle.

WHAT IF IT'S NOT STOCKINETTE STITCH?

Sometimes gauge will be given in the pattern stitch—use that for the swatch instead. It might call for ribbing, or a cable pattern, or a lace pattern. Make sure you cast on roughly twice the number of stitches called for in the gauge. For example, if the pattern says that it's expecting 18 sts and 24 rows over (k2, p2) ribbing, cast on 36 stitches and work the ribbing pattern all the way across. When you're working in a pattern stitch, no edging is required.

AND THEN MEASURE…

Once the swatch is washed and dried, measure it. Count the number of stitches and rows in 4 inches/10 cm. If it's a yarn that varies in thickness, count in a few different places to get an average.

If you're getting the right number for the pattern—congratulations! You're ready to knit. If you're getting too many stitches per 4 inches, you need a larger needle; if you're getting too few stitches, you need a smaller needle. Then start again.

Yes, you read that right. Start again. If you're more than about 10–15% off—and you like how the fabric looks and feels—you should seriously consider changing yarn. With a change in needle size, you can get about a 10% difference—e.g. if you're getting 21, you can likely get to 20 without a problem, but 18 would be pushing it.

Yes, I do go to all this trouble when I start knitting a project. Why? It's about making sure that your stitches are the right size. And stitches that are the right size means you get a garment that is the right size.

IT'S NOT JUST ABOUT SIZE

Gauge matters because fit matters. Tailors and dressmakers are very careful when they cut out fabric pieces for a garment: they pin pattern pieces down, they measure, and cut with care. When you're knitting, you're creating a piece of fabric, and to ensure that the garment fits the way you want it to, you need to make sure that your stitches are the right size. If your stitches are too big, your sweater will be too big. If your stitches are too small, your sweater will be too small. And it can be a surprisingly big problem: if you're supposed to be getting 20 sts on 4 inches, and you're getting 18, you will be gaining 4 inches around the bust on a 40 inch sweater—that's two dress sizes larger.

KATE'S PERFECT STOCKINETTE STITCH GAUGE SWATCH

Look at the gauge indicator in the pattern. It will typically be a number of stitches and rows over a 10cm/4-inch square, in stockinette stitch. If it's stated over a smaller area — for example, 1 or 2 inches, calculate the number of stitches over 4 inches.

_____ stitches x _____ rows using _____ size needles.

Using the needles specified, cast on twice that many stitches. For example, if it states 18 stitches, cast on 36.

Bottom border:
Work 6 rows in garter stitch — that is, knitting every row.

Main body:
Right side: knit entire row.
Wrong side: k3, purl to last 3 stitches, k3.
Repeat these two rows until the main body portion measures 15 cm/6 inches.

Top border:
Work 6 rows garter stitch — knitting every row. Cast off, and then wash it according to the washing instructions on the ball band for the yarn.

METRIC SIZING	US SIZE
1.5mm	000
1.75mm	00
2mm	0
2.25mm	1
2.5mm	No standard US equivalent; some patterns list as 1.5
2.75mm	2
3mm	No standard US equivalent
3.25mm	3
3.5mm	4
3.75mm	5
4mm	6
4.5mm	7

5mm	8
5.5mm	9
6mm	10
6.5mm	10½
7mm	No standard US equivalent; some patterns list as 10¾
8mm	11
9mm	13
10mm	15
12mm	17 —sometimes
12.75mm	17 - sometimes
15mm	19
19mm	35
20mm	36
25mm	50

NEEDLE SIZING — BE CAREFUL!

Although most current patterns use either metric or US sizing, there are five needle numbering systems that have been commonly used — metric, US, Canadian, English and Australian. You need to know which needle number system is being used in the pattern to make sure you're getting the right needles. A US 4 is not the same as a 4mm. When a pattern provides metric numbering, use that. It's complicated somewhat by the fact that some metric sizes don't have US equivalents.

HOW TO CHEAT

I measure the gauge of a swatch before it's washed as well as after. If it doesn't change after washing, then you know that a second swatch won't need to be washed before you measure. I also measure as I'm working—once I've got about 2 inches knit, I check the gauge. If it's way off at that point, I'll stop and restart with a different needle size.

WHY WASH?

A lot of yarns change when washed—superwash wool, for example, relaxes a fair bit; cotton can shrink up in length. It's no good having a sweater that fits well only until it's washed the first time. What this means, of course, is that the sweater might not fit when it comes off the needles—it might need to be washed before it's the proper size. That's ok—after all, every piece of knitting should be washed before it's complete! More on this in the next section.

KNITTERLY ADVICE

Don't start with a sweater. Takes too long and can get boring. Hats are much more fun and much more practical.

— Maryjean Lancefield, knitter

Swatching isn't just about size, it's also about testing out the yarn. If you're knitting a scarf, it's not going to matter if it's a bit wider (or narrower) than you intended—but you do still want to make sure it's going to look good and be fun to knit.

If I'm knitting a piece where size doesn't matter—a scarf, a blanket, a bag, for example—I will skip the step of doing a separate swatch, but I will still measure and check as I work. If, after working a few rows, you don't like how the yarn looks or feels, don't be afraid to make a change. If you don't like it early on, chances are you'll get more and more unhappy with it as the work progresses. If the yarn doesn't feel good to work with, don't be afraid to change the yarn. If you don't like how it looks—*is the yarn too fuzzy to show off the pattern stitch?* for example—don't be afraid to start again. If the fabric is too loose, start again with smaller needles; if the fabric is too stiff and tight, start again with larger needles.

KNITTERLY ADVICE

Novelty yarn is filled with promise, but it quickly loses its appeal as a knitter grows more experienced. Don't go overboard in yarn acquisition when you are in the first throes of knitting besottedness. You will quickly discover many new favorite must-haves and stash space is better reserved for yarn which does not resemble caterpillars, ladders or eyelashes.

— Wendy Setterington, knitter

Investing an hour or two in swatching and experimenting is absolutely worth it: I'd rather spend an hour and start again to get a finished result I'm truly happy with than abandon a project partway through because I hate working with the yarn. The first three or four inches of a scarf make an excellent swatch, as does the back of a baby sweater. As long as you're prepared to measure, assess and restart if you need to, go ahead and start knitting.

WILL I HAVE ENOUGH YARN?

You can assume that the designer has allowed for swatching in the given yarn requirements for a pattern, but it's always a good idea to buy an extra ball anyway. If you knit a bit longer, you'll need more yarn. If your row/round gauge is slightly off, you might use more (or less) yarn. If the cat gets into your knitting bag, you might need a bit more yarn. Hang onto your receipt—most yarn stores will take back any unused yarn in its original packaging for store credit. If you're not sure, ask before you buy. Stores are likely to be more willing to take returns on recently purchased, full-price yarn. If the yarn is on sale, chances are you won't be able to return or exchange it. In that situation, buy two extra balls and if there are leftovers, make a hat!

GET YOUR EQUIPMENT TOGETHER

TOOLS

Get everything together in your knitting bag or basket: all the yarn and the tools listed on the pattern, e.g. stitch markers, stitch holders, cable needles, darning needle. See page 29 for a list of my favorites!

THE PATTERN

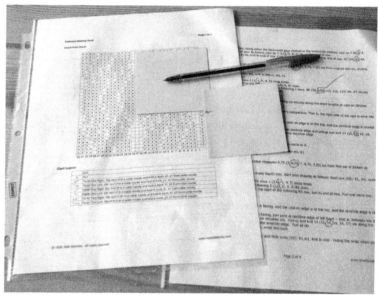

As mentioned in the previous section, always look for updates and errata before you begin. For online patterns, download/print the most recent version. For a pattern in a book or magazine, search Google. Look it up on Ravelry to see if there are any comments, and print those out, too.

If it's from a book or a magazine, make a photocopy, and put the original away somewhere safe. If it's online, print a second copy. If you spill coffee on your working copy, you'll be ok. You can mark up the working copy to your heart's content: cross off sections as you go, make notes on changes you might have made, keep track of stitch and row counts.

Go through the pattern and circle the numbers for your size. It makes it easier to keep track of what you're doing—it's surprisingly easy to misread a number, especially when there are lots of sizes in the pattern. And of course, if you put the project down for a while, it will help you find your way when you start working on it again.

Keep the working copy of the pattern in a plastic sheet protector—it keeps the sheet clean and dry (in case of coffee spills), and makes it easier to find in your knitting bag. Folded up sheets of paper get lost very easily. A pro tip from my good friend Lynne: If you're using sticky notes, make sure you put them in the right place on the *inside* of the sheet protector when you put your knitting away, so that they don't fall off or get lost. If you're marking your position in a chart, you may want to use highlighter tape (available at office supply stores). For long rows or repeats you haven't finished, mark the place you ended on the highlighter tape so you know where to pick up when you knit again.

Chapter 3: Working From a Pattern

GENERAL GUIDELINES

FIND THE GLOSSARY

Before you begin, it's a good idea to locate the glossary or table of abbreviations. Sometimes it's right in the pattern, especially if it's a pattern published individually. If the pattern comes from a book or magazine, it's usually in the back somewhere. Online pattern publishers often maintain a single page with the abbreviations—Knitty, for example, has its "Knitty Standard Book of British Birds" (it's an old Monty Python joke) on the pattern index page.

US TERM	UK TERM
Bind off	*Cast off*
Gauge	*Tension*
Stockinette stitch	*Stocking stitch*
Yarnover, yarn over	*Yarn forward*

It's not a bad idea to print out or copy the glossary when you print out the pattern—*and keep it with you.* Abbreviations aren't entirely standardized. Although there are a bunch that are fairly obvious and common —k means knit and p means purl, for example— don't assume that you know what they all mean. In some contexts, for example, k1b means 'knit 1 stitch in the back of the loop,' and in other contexts it means 'knit one stitch in the row below.'

In addition, language varies slightly between US and UK patterns—and Canadian patterns tend to sit somewhere in the middle using a combination of the two.

Some patterns like to use different words to mean the same thing... for example, *grafting* is another term for Kitchener stitch. Some patterns will say "pick up," others will say "pick up and knit." And a lot of patterns will have a special Notes section—often placed helpfully at the start. This is where pattern-specific terms and techniques will be explained. In particular, for cable patterns, all sorts of non-standard terms might be used (e.g., C4F, TW2) and a pattern should always provide definitions. When in doubt on a term or abbreviation, don't panic—just look for pattern notes and check the glossary.

TAKE NOTES

If you're using different size needles than those suggested in the pattern (and you'll have swatched, so you know what size needles to use), write that down on the pattern.

If you make changes—for example, if you're using black and white for stripes instead of the blue and red shown in the pattern, make sure you write down which color you are substituting for which. If the stripes are the same width, then it won't matter if you mix them up, but if the blue stripes are wider than the red, you need to make sure you stay consistent in which color you use when.

When you put the knitting down at the end of the evening, or as the train pulls into the station, make a quick note of where you were. It's much easier to start knitting again the next time if you know where you left off.

WORK THE SECTIONS IN THE ORDER THEY ARE WRITTEN

There may well be a specific reason it's written that way: for example, many pullover patterns have you work the body partway through, stop, knit the sleeves, and then continue.

Check the sections off as you go. I've seen a cardigan knitted with two left fronts because the knitter got confused about which pieces she had already knitted.

TAKE A GOOD LOOK

Before you pick up your knitting for the evening, as you're settling onto the couch, pull your knitting out of its bag and examine it. If you're working in low light in front of the TV, make sure you switch the light on and really *look* at it before you put it away for the night. Every so often as you work, hold up your knitting and take a gander. Take a moment to admire your work, and to check to make sure things are going ok.

Count your stitches. Check for dropped stitches. Check to see if you're working on the correct side. (It's easy to mix up the RS and WS, trust me.)

Check to see if the piece you're knitting is roughly the shape and size you expect it to be. Check to make sure you've only made two sleeves, and one right front and one left front.

If you're working stripes on the sleeves, look at the first one to see which color you started with before casting on for the second.

Place the front and back against each other to make sure that the back is the same length as the front. Compare the second sock with the first to make sure they are the same size.

If you're working with straight needles, make sure you're knitting with a matched set. (If a project needs more than one size of needle, and they are all in your knitting bag, be very careful to pick up the right ones.)

After all, the sooner you spot a mistake, the easier it is to fix. And if it's all going well, you can enjoy and admire your progress!

> ## KNITTERLY ADVICE
>
> *I received a great pin one day from a knitter who knows me well saying 'My gauge is fine til the third glass of wine'... I'm not going to stop knitting at the pub, but I know better than to take anything difficult with me!*
>
> *— Jennifer Campbell, LYS owner*

READING THE INSTRUCTIONS

GARTER STITCH AND STOCKINETTE STITCH

These are the two most common stitch patterns, and quite often they are not specifically written out in a pattern. The designer just assumes you know what it means. For example, a pattern might just say to work "5 inches in garter stitch", or "12 rows of stockinette stitch".

*   **GARTER STITCH:** *Knit every row.*
*   **STOCKINETTE STITCH:** *Row 1 [RS]: Knit. Row 2 [WS]: Purl.*
*   **REVERSE STOCKINETTE STITCH:** Stockinette stitch but with purls as the right side rows. *Row 1 [RS]: Purl. Row 2 [WS]: Knit.*

Note: Things are intriguingly different for garter stitch and stockinette stitch when you're working in the round. See Chapter 7 for more information.

RIBBING

I remember very clearly my first attempt to tackle ribbing. Of course, it makes perfect sense: (k1, p1) ribbing means that I am to knit one stitch and purl the next. It took me two days to get the first row right, and then another couple of days to get the second row correct.

The instructions say glibly to knit 1 stitch and purl the next... but I (like millions of other knitters) didn't realize that I had to move the yarn between the stitches. To knit, the yarn should be at the back; to purl, the yarn should be at the front. And so after a knit and before a purl, the yarn needs to be moved to the front. And after a purl and before a knit, the yarn needs to be moved to the back. If you don't you get a giant mess with the yarn looped back and forth over the needle every time you switch stitches.

So yes, if your ribbing doesn't work out, make sure you are remembering to move the yarn between the stitches!

And the other problem is that the first row might be easy, but what you do on the second row depends on what ribbing pattern you're doing, and how many stitches you have. Designers will often take a shortcut with the instructions. Sometimes the instructions will just say to work (k1, p1) ribbing. Sometimes, they will provide the additional instruction to "knit the knits and purl the purls". And indeed, this is the principle: when working ribbing, you're stacking knits on top of knits, and purls on top of purls.

Ribbing comes in all sorts of combinations: (k1, p1), (k2, p2), (k3, p3), and so forth. And there's no rule that you need to knit the same number of stitches you purl: (k3, p1) is one of my favorite ribbings for use in socks.

K1, P1 RIBBING

Row 1 [RS]: (K1, p1) to end.

If you have an even number of stitches, Row 2 is exactly the same.
If you have an odd number of stitches, Row 2 is different:

(P1, k1) until 1 st rems, p1.

This works because if you have an even number of stitches, then the RS row ends with a purl. And remembering that the purl is the reverse of a knit, that first stitch will then show as a knit stitch on the other side, so the second row again is worked as (k1, p1) all the way across.

If you've got an odd number of stitches, then you start and end the first row with a k1. And since that k1 on the RS shows as a p1 on the WS, you start the WS row with a p1. And because it's an odd number of stitches, the WS row ends with a p1, also.

K2, P2 RIBBING:

The first row is again easy:

Row 1 [RS]: (K2, p2) to end.

How you start Row 2 depends on how many stitches you have. If you have a multiple of 4, then Row 2 is the same.
If you end Row 1 with p1 rather than p2, then Row 2 starts with K1 rather than k2. If you end Row 1 with 1 or 2 knits, then you will start with 1 or 2 purl stitches.

So for any ribbing, if you have an exact multiple of the number of stitches in the ribbing pattern—6 for (k3, p3), for example, then every row is the same. Otherwise you have to adjust the pattern on the second row to compensate. And it's easy from there, as any ribbing is just a two-row pattern.

No matter what ribbing pattern you're working, once you're a few rows in, you won't need to count anymore—the stitches will tell you what needs to be done: knit the knits and purl the purls.

SEED STITCH AND MOSS STITCH:

In general, in the UK, moss stitch is the same as the US seed stitch, and worked as follows, on an even number of stitches:

Row 1 [RS]: [K1, p1], repeat to end.
Row 2 [WS]: [P1, k1], repeat to end.

Seed stitch is just "broken" (k1, p1) ribbing: purl the knits and knit the purls. And US moss stitch is the same as UK double moss stitch, worked as follows, again on an even number of stitches:

Rows 1 and 2: [K1, p1], repeat to end.
Row 3 and 4: [P1, k1], repeat to end.

You're working 2 rows of (k1, p1) ribbing, then two rows of the alternate ribbing, (p1, k1).

BRACKETS AND ASTERISKS:

Brackets and asterisks are used to indicate repeats. For example, a pattern might say:

Cast on 78 stitches.
*Row 1 [RS]: *K2, p2; repeat from * to last 2 sts, k2.*

KNITTERLY ADVICE

Swatching is an excellent use of a knitter's time. If it sounds too much like work, try to think of it as 'doodling with yarn.'

— Cynthia MacDougall, Canadian Guild of Knitters

This means that you keep doing what's between the asterisk and the semicolon until there are only 2 stitches left in the row, and then you just do what it tells you for that last 2 sts. Sometimes, it might look like this:

> Row 1 [RS]: *K2, p2*, repeat between ** to last 2 sts, k2.
> or: Row 1 [RS]: [K2, p2] to last 2 sts, k2.

They all mean the same thing—just keep doing whatever it tells you to until you get to the last 2 stitches.

HOW MANY TIMES?

Look for the word "more". When you're repeating an instruction over and over again, pay attention to how it's written. For example:

> Row 1 [RS]: Knit.
> Row 2 [WS]: Purl.
> Repeat the above two rows 9 more times.

The use of the word "more" is the key here. This means that you work 20 rows in total—the first two, and then the same two again 9 more times—that's another 18 rows, for 20 in total. But if, instead, it says "Work the above two rows 9 times", it means that you only work 18 rows.

PAY ATTENTION TO THE NUMBERS

A pattern will often list a stitch count after a row or a set of instructions. This is the designer's way of telling you that it's a good idea to count your stitches at this point. After all, the next section may well require a specific number of stitches—check before you move on.

KEY WORDS & PHRASES

RIGHT SIDE: The side of the knitting that will be showing—the public side, if you will. It's usually the prettier side.

WRONG SIDE: The inside of the garment, the private side.

"LEFT" AND "RIGHT": In a garment pattern, this means from the wearer's perspective.

"NECKLINE EDGE" AND "ARMHOLE EDGE": It can be easy to mix these two up in a garment pattern. If it doubt, lay the piece out and figure out how it will fit on your body.

> **DIRTY SECRET**
>
> *It's absolutely critical to match stitch gauge. There is no such thing as "close enough." But for most applications, there is a little room for fudging in row/round gauge. If you're off by a row or two, don't worry about it. Most garments are written to have you work to a certain length, so it won't matter if you work a few rows more or less than the designer did. But if you're off by more than about 10% (e.g. 2 rows in 20), that's a sign that your yarn is probably not the right one.*

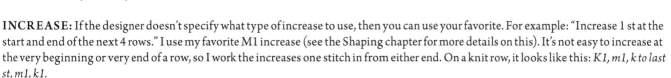

Neckline edge

Armhole edge

INCREASE: If the designer doesn't specify what type of increase to use, then you can use your favorite. For example: "Increase 1 st at the start and end of the next 4 rows." I use my favorite M1 increase (see the Shaping chapter for more details on this). It's not easy to increase at the very beginning or very end of a row, so I work the increases one stitch in from either end. On a knit row, it looks like this: *K1, m1, k to last st, m1, k1.*

DECREASE: If the designer doesn't specific what type of decrease to use, then you can use your favorite. For example: "Decrease 1 st at each end of the next 4 rows." If you're working in stockinette, and your first row is a knit, k2tog works very well at both ends. If you're on a purl row, p2tog is perfect (see the Shaping chapter for more details). If the designer has a specific decrease in mind, she'll tell you.

If you put the decreases right at the ends of the row on a garment that is going to be seamed up, e.g. *K2tog, k to last 2 sts, k2tog,* the decreases will be hidden in the seams, but it will make sewing up a little bit more challenging. If you put the decreases one or two stitches in from the ends of the row, then the decreases will be visible, but sewing up will be easier, e.g. *K2, k2tog, k to last 4 sts, k2tog, k2.*

EVEN: You typically see this after a set of increases and decreases. Think of this as a reset: it means that you stop the shaping, and now just proceed with the number of stitches you have. For example:

> *Row 12 [RS]: K2tog, k9. 10 stitches.*
> *Row 13 [WS]: K8, k2tog. 9 stitches.*
> *Work even until piece measures 4 inches.*

So, you will just knit those 9 stitches until the piece is 4 inches long.

IN PATTERN AS ESTABLISHED: or sometimes just "As established" means that you are to keep doing what you've been doing. For example:

> *Row 1 [RS]: (K1, p1), repeat to end.*
> *Row 2 [WS]: (P1, k1), repeat to end.*
> *Continue as established until piece measures 10 inches.*

This means to just keep repeating these two rows until the piece is the right length.

ENDING WITH WS (OR RS) ROW: This is telling you where to stop. For example, a pattern might say "Work 10 inches in stockinette stitch, ending with a WS row." This means that the last row you work should be a WS row.

WITH RS (OR WS) FACING: This is telling you where you need to be—what side you need to be looking at when you start the next row (or section). If you finished a section ending with WS, the RS would be facing for the next section—that is, you're looking at the RS, ready to work it.

EVERY FOLL ALT ROW: "Foll" is short for following. "Alt" is short for alternate. So if a pattern says "Decrease at each end of every foll alt row," it just means that you decrease at the start and end of every *other* row from here, until it tells you to stop. For example:

> *Decrease row [RS]: K2tog, k to last 2 sts, k2tog.*
> *Continuing in stockinette, decrease at both ends of every foll alt row to 10 sts.*

So what you'd do here is purl the WS rows, and repeat the decrease on every other row—every RS row—until you have 10 stitches. Use your paper and pencil to help you keep track.

EVERY 6TH ROW 10 TIMES: This means that you're to do something every 6th row, and you're going to do that 10 times. For example:

> *Decrease row [RS]: K2tog, k to last 2 sts, k2tog.*
> *Continuing in stockinette, work decrease every 6th row 10 times.*

Here's how this goes: Work a decrease row as written, then 5 rows even (WS/purl, RS/knit, WS/purl, RS/knit, WS/purl). You now reach the 6th row, so you repeat the decrease row. And then work another five even rows, and another decrease row, and repeat that pattern until 10 decrease rows have been worked. You'll work 55 rows in total—(1 decrease row, 5 even rows) 9 times, then 1

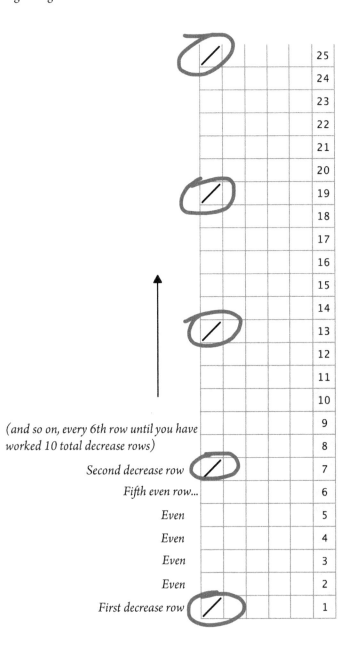

(and so on, every 6th row until you have worked 10 total decrease rows)

Second decrease row

Fifth even row...

Even

Even

Even

Even

First decrease row

decrease row more. I find it's helpful to write out a little chart to help me keep track of this. See sample at right.

AT THE START OF THE NEXT 2 ROWS: You see this most commonly when shaping the armholes in a garment. It's done this way because binding off at the end of a row forces you to cut and rejoin the yarn. Try it—your yarn gets stranded on that last stitch and you can't knit back. The instruction might say "bind off 4 sts at the start of the next 2 rows." It's quite literal: bind off 4 sts, then work to end. On the following row, bind off 4 more, and work to end. It's true that one side will be a row longer than the other before the bind off, but the difference is imperceptible in the finished product.

INCREASE STS EVENLY ACROSS: If the designer uses this type of instruction, it means that she doesn't have a specific requirement in mind for what type of increase to use, or where the increases should go. I always use my favorite M1 for this sort of instruction (see the Shaping chapter). For example: *Increase 5 sts evenly across the 60 sts of current row.*

You've got 60 stitches, and you need to increase to 65. So, $60 \div 5 = 12$. This means that you work 12 sts between increases. You can think of it as the following: [K12, m1] 5 times.

If you're working in the round, that's perfectly even. If you're working flat, you need to make a small adjustment since you don't want an increase at the end of the row. I take that first group of 12 stitches, and stick half of them at the end of the row. This gives me k6, m1, [k12, m1] 4 times, k6. Much more even!

What if the number of stitches doesn't divide evenly? For example: Increase 5 sts evenly across the 68 sts of current row.

$68 \div 5 = 13.6$ stitches.

So the basic pattern is *[K13, m1] 5 times*, which adds up to 65 sts, and then work the extra 3 sts at the end of the row:

[K13, m1] 5 times, k3.

And if you want to make it tidy around the edges, even up the stitches at the edges. You've got 13 at the start before the first increase, and 3 at the end after the last.

$13 + 3 = 16$
$16 \div 2 = 8$

So you need 8 sts before the first increase, and 8 stitches after the last.

K8, m1, [k13, m1] 4 times, k8.

If I'm doing any of these types of increases, I always write the row out, and I do a quick check of my math by counting the m1s to make sure I have enough. I also count the resulting stitches, including the m1. If you're more visually-oriented, you may want to draw the row instead.

KATE'S FAVORITE TOOLS

These are the things I keep in my knitting bag at all times:

- *safety pins*
- *stitch markers*
- *stitch holders and/or giant safety pins*
- *scissors*
- *a ruler*
- *needle gauge*
- *tape measure*
- *notebook and pencil*
- *a crochet hook (for picking up dropping stitches)*

A pencil, a few sheets of lined paper, and some sticky notes are incredibly useful, too.

DIRTY SECRET

Sometimes it doesn't work out exactly. Sometimes you might have more stitches at one end than the other. Sometimes you might lose count and get to the end without having worked the expected number of stitches. Remember, if the designer didn't specify precisely where to put the increases, you don't need to worry about it too much. As long as you've got the right number of stitches when you're done with the row, you're good.

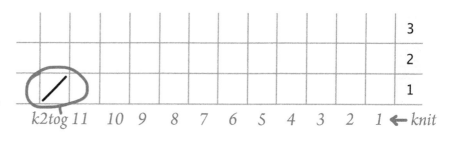

DECREASE STITCHES EVENLY ACROSS: As above, if the designer uses this type of instruction, it means that she doesn't have a specific requirement in mind for what type of decrease to use or where the decrease should go. Decreasing is different than increasing, though (See the Shaping chapter for more details on this). For example: *Decrease 5 sts evenly across the 65 sts of current row.*

$$65 \div 5 = 13$$

So you've got 5 groups of 13 stitches—and you need to work a decrease in each group of 13 sts—which means *[K11, k2tog] 5 times*. And as before, divide up the stitches at the start of the row to make it nice and tidy which gives you *K6, k2tog, [k11, k2tog] 4 times, k5*. Or thereabouts!

As with the increase version, if I'm doing any of these types of decreases, I always write the row out and I do a quick check of my math, and as long as I get to the right number of stitches at the end, I don't worry too much.

SPECIAL SITUATIONS

WORKING FROM CHARTS

Some pattern stitches are charted—lace and cables, most commonly. Charts are simply another way of representing a stitch pattern, nothing more. Any written instructions can be represented in a chart, any chart can be written out. As to which you prefer, it's not about your talent or experience as a knitter, or your level of intelligence—it's all about your learning style. Visual learners or those who are good at pattern recognition tend to prefer charts; auditory learners tend to prefer written instructions. One isn't better or more proper than the other, they are just different.

Sometimes you'll get both in a pattern, sometimes, only one. And often, the one that the pattern uses is a reflection of which one the designer herself prefers—nothing more!

First things first, locate the legend. That's the key—pun intended. Every chart will have a legend—whether on the same page or at the end of the book or magazine. On page 124 is the legend for patterns in this book. Always make sure you find it—not all symbols are standardized. Don't worry, though, you'll never have to guess. If the designer doesn't have a complete legend, or is forcing you to guess, this is a yet another sign that this pattern may not be the right one for you! See right for a sample chart legend.

Then look at the numbers at the top—that tells you that this is worked over 7 stitches. And the numbers on the sides are the row numbers—there are 16 rows in total. The row numbers are the clues to how the chart is read. Row 1, which is a RS row, is read from right to left. All RS rows are read from right to left. Row 2 (and all following even-numbered rows) are WS rows, and they are read from left to right.

Think about a row of 7 stitches. You knit them in order: stitch 1, 2, 3, 4, 5, 6, 7. When you turn around to work back, you start with stitch 7, and work back to stitch 1. So charts are read in the direction you knit.

Let's take a look at the Legend. The last three symbols are easy, but there's something funny going on with the first one. A blank square like this ☐ has two definitions: knit on the RS and purl on the WS.

> Row 1 is a RS row, so it goes like this: *P1, ssk, k3, yo, p1*.
> Row 2 is a WS row, so it goes like this: *K1, p5, k1*.

Why change the meaning? It's because a chart is a picture of the front of your knitting. Really, a blank square like this ☐ means "do whatever you need to do so that the stitch shows as a knit on the RS." And a knit on the RS is a purl on the WS. The dot also has two definitions – do

---

DIRTY SECRET

Reversing shaping: the internet can be your friend! Before you start to do the work, do a quick search for the pattern on Ravelry. Knitters often write out the instructions and post them on Ravelry to help our their fellow knitters.

	7	6	5	4	3	2	1	
16	●						●	
	●	/	O				●	15
14	●						●	
	●	/		O			●	13
12	●						●	
	●	/			O		●	11
10	●						●	
	●	/				O	●	9
8	●						●	
	●				O	\	●	7
6	●						●	
	●			O		\	●	5
4	●						●	
	●		O			\	●	3
2	●						●	
	●	O				\	●	1

LEGEND

●	**purl**	RS: purl WS: knit
\	**ssk**	RS: slip one stitch as if to knit. Slip another stitch as if to knit. Insert left hand needle into front of these two stitches and knit them together.
☐	**knit**	RS: knit WS: purl
O	**yo**	Yarn over
/	**k2tog**	RS: Knit two stitches together as one stitch

what you need to do so that the stitch shows as a purl on the RS. The other three symbols only have one definition since they are only worked on the RS. This way, you can easily look at your knitting and compare it with the chart, and you'll see they have a certain resemblance.

Some charts only show the RS rows—the row numbers will be the clue here: if a chart only has rows 1, 3, 5... and so forth, only the RS rows have been charted. Look for some text near the chart—or in the instructions where it first mentions the chart—that describes what to do on the WS rows. This is sometimes done to make the charts smaller and easier to read, and you can assume that the WS rows are all going to be the same.

No matter which you prefer, you're going to encounter a pattern that doesn't have the one you like. If you find you prefer written instructions, feel free to write the rows out before you begin; if you prefer charts, you may want to draw charts for the written instructions. Use whichever you find easiest!

(For information on working charts in the round, see "Working in the Round" on page 54).

AT THE SAME TIME

It's an innocent little phrase, but one you need to look out for. I always read through a pattern before I start working, and this is one of the key reasons I do. If I see the words "AT THE SAME TIME," I underline them, put exclamation marks around them, and maybe even get out my favorite yellow highlighter.

All it means is that partway through one set of instructions, you need to do something else. For example:

> *Dec 1 st each end of next and every foll 6th row, 10 times. AT THE SAME TIME, when piece measures 13.5 [13.5, 14] inches, change to [K1, p1] Rib Pattern.*

It looks scary, but it's not. You're working some decreases—a pattern of decreasing every 6th row, and at some stage during those decreases, the back is going to hit the right length. And when it hits that length, you need to change to the ribbing pattern. The decreases won't stop, you'll just change the stitch pattern you're working while doing the 6-row decreases. What this means, practically, is that as you're working those decrease rows, keep measuring to make sure you know when you reach the required length. You might reach the right length on a decrease row, you might reach it on one of the even rows—it doesn't matter, just change to ribbing when you get to the right point, and keep the decrease pattern going.

REVERSING SHAPING

This phrase strikes fear in the heart of many knitters, but it needn't be so. A bit of care is all that's required. Now, any pattern that has this phrase is not a beginner pattern—and any pattern that claims to be easy that uses this phrase isn't playing fair. Another good reason to read through before you begin!

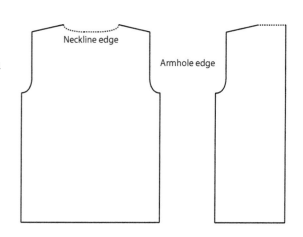

Neckline edge

Armhole edge

This is usually a sign that a pattern has been edited down for space—when you're doing the same thing on two pieces that are mirror images of each other. The most common place you see it is on the neckline of a sweater. The key when working a pattern that uses this is to write down what you do on the first side so you can duplicate it on the second. For example:

> *Shape Front Necklines:*
> *72 [88, 104] sts. With RS facing, k 34 [42, 50] sts, K2tog, turn.*
> *Cont on the left side of front only, dec 1 st at neck edge on every row until there are 18 [24, 30]sts on the needle. Work even to 5 [5.5, 6] inches from beg. of shaping.*
> *Shape Shoulder:*
> *BO 6 [8, 10] sts at shoulder edge 3 times. Work the right side of front as for left, reversing shapings.*

As you work, write down what you do: with RS facing, you will knit across to 2 sts short of the center point, and k2tog, and then turn. This is the left side of the front. The pattern tells you to continue in stockinette stitch on those stitches only, and work a decrease every row on the neck edge.

On the Left Front, the neck edge is at the end of the RS rows, and the start of the WS rows. Write this down! You start with a WS row because you've just worked a RS row.

So you'll work as follows:

> *WS rows: P2tog, p to end.*
> *RS rows: K to last 2 sts, k2tog.*

And keep repeating these two rows until you have decreased to the right number of stitches (18 [24, 30], depending on which size you're working). Then work even until the piece is as long as you need (5 [5.5, 6] inches, depending on which size you're working). At this point, you will bind off at the shoulder edge—this is the opposite side from the neck edge. So on the Left Front, it's at the start of the RS rows, and the end of the WS rows. Write this down! And remembering that you can only bind off at the start of a row, it goes like this:

> *Row 1 [RS]: Bind off 6 [8, 10] sts, k to end.*
> *Row 2 [WS]: Purl.*
> *Row 3 [RS]: Bind off 6 [8, 10] sts, k to end.*
> *Row 4 [WS]: Purl.*
> *Row 5 [RS]: Bind off 6 [8, 10] sts—and then you're done!*

And because you've written down the key info, the other side is easy. The neck and shoulder edges are at the other sides from the Left Front.

	Neckline Edge	Shoulder Edge
Left Front	End of RS, start of WS.	Start of RS, end of WS.
Right Front	Start of RS, end of WS.	End of RS, start of WS.

Right Front:

You'll rejoin the yarn where you left off—at the neck edge of the Right Front.

> *Row 1 [RS]: K2tog, k to end.*

This matches the very first decrease you did on the Left Front.

On the Right Front, the neck edge is at the start of the RS rows, and the end of the WS rows. You start with a WS row because you've just worked a RS row.

So you'll work as follows:

> *WS rows: P to last 2 sts, p2tog.*
> *RS rows: K2tog, k to end.*

...and keep repeating these two rows until you have the right number of stitches 18 [24, 30], depending on which size you're working. Then, work even until the piece is as long as you need, and next you will bind off at the shoulder edge. This is the opposite side from the neck edge, so on the Right Front, it's at the end of the RS rows, and the start of the WS rows. And remembering that you can only bind off at the start of a row, it goes like this:

(Make sure you have the WS facing!)

> *Row 1 [WS]: Bind off 6 [8, 10] sts, p to end.*
> *Row 2 [RS]: K.*
> *Row 3 [WS]: Bind off 6 [8, 10] sts, p to end.*
> *Row 4 [RS]: K.*
> *Row 5 [WS]: Bind off 6 [8, 10] sts—and then you're done.*

Chapter 4: What Patterns Don't Tell You

JOINING A NEW BALL OF YARN

Oh boy, I remember this well: I was knitting up a storm on my first scarf, and when I hit the end of the first ball of yarn I stopped dead. I had bought two balls of yarn to make a good long scarf but quickly realized I hadn't the faintest idea how to join the new one.

What you need to do depends on whether you're knitting something in one piece, like a scarf, or whether it's going to be sewn up. If it's a one piece item like a scarf—where the edges are going to be exposed—it's better to join the new ball in the middle of the row. Lay the two strands together—as if the new ball were the continuation of the old one—leaving about a 4-inch tail on both, and work three stitches with both ends of the yarn.

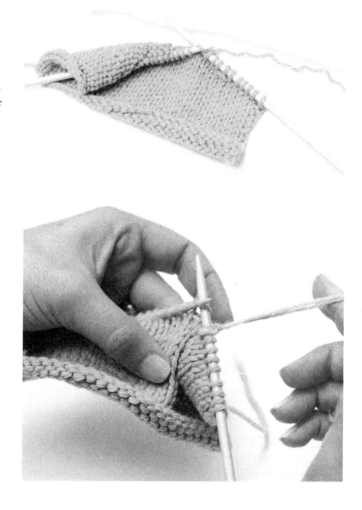

In the pictures at right I've used two different colors so you can see how it works. This does thicken up these three stitches somewhat, but it's barely visible in the final result, and makes for a very tidy and secure join. When working these stitches on the next row, just remember that even if the stitch has two strands, it's still just one stitch. When the piece is complete, weave in your ends. See below for information on that.

If the piece is going to be seamed up, then change yarn at the end of the row. Drop the old end, and tie the new one on, with a simple overhand knot. The knot isn't about security, it's about positioning—the two ends are tied together, so they stay close and snug, ensuring that the last stitch of the old yarn and the first stitch of the new yarn stay tidy and even.

How do you know if you have enough yarn to finish a row? You need about three row-widths in yarn to knit across the row. If you're close to running out, err on the side of caution and change yarn sooner rather than later.

SEAMING & WEAVING IN ENDS

I cover specific key seaming techniques in later pages, but the main thing to know is this: sewing up knitting is totally different than sewing up fabric. If you know anything about sewing fabric, throw it out before you begin.

A proper seam for knitted fabrics takes a little bit longer than a "sewing" seam, but it looks so much better—it's absolutely worth it. First of all: you seam knitting with the right (public) sides facing you. Sewing up knitting is sometimes referred to as "weaving" in older books, and it's an accurate way of describing it—you create the seam by weaving a strand of yarn through the edges of the pieces. And indeed, using the ends for seaming is the best way of weaving in the tails from your cast ons and bind offs.

Older knitting books, and some knitters of the WWII generation will tell you that you shouldn't use your ends to seam. This advice dates back to times when yarn was a very scarce resource—it's harder to undo your knitting if you've used your tails for sewing up. But if you're not planning to undo the sweater, save yourself some extra work and seam with the tails!

DIRTY SECRET

Spit splicing: If your yarn is feltable—that is, a non-superwash animal fiber—you can felt the two ends together for a totally invisible join. Fray about two inches of each of the two yarn ends by splitting the plies, then overlap the ends. Get the yarns soaking wet—spit works best, but water is good, too—and aggressively rub them between your hands to felt them together. Once it dries, you've got a strong and invisible join—and two fewer ends to weave in.

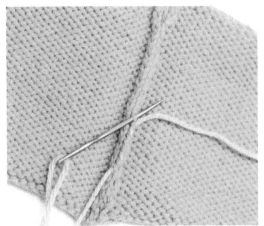

Weaving end into seam

Weaving ends diagonally

Note, however, that you don't *need* to use the yarn you knitted with for seaming—proper seaming methods hide the seaming yarn! And some yarn just isn't appropriate. If it's a delicate yarn, not very tightly spun, it will fray and shred as you seam.

Choose a smooth, colorfast yarn that's got the same washability characteristics as the yarn you used. Don't seam a machine-washable sweater with a yarn that felts. I've done it; it makes a terrible mess and an unwearable sweater. Sock yarn is terrific for seaming, as it's strong, washable, colorfast, and you get miles of it for very little money.

The great thing about a seam is it's the best place to weave in your ends; you don't have to be very tidy about it, and they will never be visible from the right side. Thread a blunt-ended darning needle with your end and run it up and down the seam.

If you haven't got a seam—as in a scarf, for example—you'll need to weave the ends in the middle of your piece. Thread a blunt-ended darning needle with your end and weave it diagonally across the back of the work, picking up the purl loops. Go in a couple of different directions. (If you weave vertically, it will pop through to the right side, and if you weave horizontally, you're putting a row under pressure, and it can cause a visible pucker.)

No matter where you're weaving the ends in, make sure you're burying about 3–4 inches of yarn. Before you trim the excess off, pull the work to seat the stitches naturally, and then snip.

MEASURING

A pattern will often have you working to a certain distance—*12 inches before the armhole shaping*, for example, or *2 inches between buttonholes*, or *6 inches before the decreases start*. To get an accurate measurement, use a high-quality tape measure and lay the item flat. Those paper tape measures you get at that Scandinavian furniture store? They rip. That old fabric tape measure you bought at a garage sale for 25 cents? It may well have stretched. The rusty metal tape measure you found in a toolbox in the garage? Not flexible enough. A ruler? Not long enough. A good tape measure from a sewing or knitting shop is what you need.

Place your knitting flat—on a flat surface—to measure. Knitting can sag and stretch if you hang it to measure, and it will definitely stretch if you try to put it over your leg or the arm of your sofa.

Remember that if your swatch stretched significantly in length when you washed it, you should take that into account in the measurement. If it stretched 10% (to get the right gauge), knit 10% shorter—9 inches rather than 10, for example.

When a piece comes off my needles, I like to measure it and compare it against the schematic—it is roughly the same size and shape as the piece in the schematic? It's a good sanity check. And if I'm making two of the same thing—sleeves, for example—I like to measure them against each other to check I'm on track.

Some knitters take a very practical approach: if they are knitting two pieces that must be precisely the same length—sleeves, for example—they knit them at the same time. They use a longer circular needle, with a separate ball of yarn attached to each piece. What you lose in portability of the project, you gain in accuracy.

WHAT TO DO IF IT'S NOT GOING WELL

It happens! Things go wrong. We get bored. We get off track. Sometimes, it's the right thing to put your knitting down and work on something else instead.

If you're not enjoying working on a project, take a break. It might be that it's just not the right project for *now*. When I'm very busy with writing and editing work, I tend to prefer simpler knitting that doesn't require so much attention; when I'm feeling creative, I tend to enjoy challenging knitting like lace or complex cable patterns. Give yourself permission to change projects if you need to. You may well find that in a week or two, it's exactly the thing you want to be knitting.

> ## KNITTERLY ADVICE
>
> *Don't simply follow the pattern, try to understand the pattern. The sooner you get the big picture, the sooner you will know if something's not right. Mistakes are so much easier to fix if you catch them right away.*
>
> *— Julie Stewart, knitter*

What if you're not enjoying the yarn? Finding it itchy, or difficult to work with? If you've swatched with the yarn, you'll have a good sense of whether you like it or not. If you hate the yarn, chances are you won't want to wear the finished item—consider changing yarn.

What if you hate the garment? Is it going to be too big or too small even after your careful swatching? What if you don't like the way it looks? Give yourself a break—better to abandon a project after two hours than slog through the entire project hating every step, and then never even wear the result. I never felt guilty about stopping a project after a couple of hours—I just make a note of what I didn't enjoy about it, and used that knowledge to ensure I pick projects I know I'll love in the future. Sometimes, the best thing you can do with a project is put it down and work on something else. Onwards to better things!

WASH IT WHEN YOU'RE DONE—OR WHAT THE HECK IS THIS BLOCKING BUSINESS ALL ABOUT?

I never declare a project finished until it's been washed and dried. It's essential if you're going to be doing any seaming. If pieces are going to stretch or shrink that needs to happen before you sew up so the seams don't pucker. But even if it's not going to be seamed, washing a piece makes it look so much better. The stitches even out and the surface gets smoother. And chances are, the yarn you worked with is pretty dirty—as it moves from the mill to packaging to shipping and to the yarn shop, yarns gather machine oils from the spinning, dust from the mill air, other fiber strands and fluff from the yarn shop, and lint from whatever else it's been stored with (in other words: it probably wasn't perfectly clean even when you first bought it). Not to mention that as you knit it, it might gather coffee stains, pet hair, cookie crumbs. In short, after a good wash, you knitting just looks better. Try it next time you knit two of something—socks, mitts, sleeves. Wash one and compare it against the other. You'll be very pleasantly surprised.

In fact, this is what blocking is. For most things, when a pattern says to block, all that needs to happen is to wash it. The only type of knitting that needs special blocking treatment is lace; lace requires stretching to open up the stitchwork and make it look its best.

> ## WHY NOT KNOTS?
>
> *Knitters are often told to avoid making knots, but often without the explanation. It's not that they are morally wrong in some way, but they're unhelpful. Knots do two things knitters don't like. First, if you cut the ends short, they invariably come undone. Second, if you have a knot on the inside of your garment, it will tend to pop through to the outside for all to see.*
>
> *A knot at the edge is ok because, first of all you're not going to cut the ends short—at least I've just told you not to—and because they'll be hidden in the seam and won't be able to work their way through to the right side.*
>
> *If you encounter a knot in a ball of yarn as you work, break the yarn and treat it like you're joining a new ball.*

Washing is absolutely the best way to block. Neither pressing nor steam blocking can be fully guaranteed to take care of whatever stretching or shrinking is going to happen; and pressing can flatten out your knitting too much—for example, pressing an Aran sweater squishes up all that lovely cabling.

Do wash it according to the washing instructions on the ball band for the yarn—handwash or machine wash. I tend to air dry most things, even if they are dryer-safe—it saves energy and wear-and-tear on the garment. If you're air-drying, find somewhere you can lay the items flat.

Chapter 5: Other Frequently Asked Questions

CONTINENTAL KNITTING AND ENGLISH KNITTING

These aren't political or geographic designations; they're simply different ways of holding your yarn. "English" knitting is when you hold your yarn in your right hand; "Continental" knitting is when you hold your yarn in your left hand.

They are utterly interchangeable; the instructions are no different, and the patterns are worked precisely the same. It's sort of like writing with the pen in your left versus your right hand—it looks different while you're doing it, but what results is identical.

Which method knitters prefer tends to depend on a few things—which method a knitter learned first, how long the knitter has been working that way, how strongly right- or left-handed a knitter is. If a knitter hasn't been working one way or the other very long, the habit won't be deeply ingrained, and so it's easier to switch. Me, I'm very strongly right-handed, and pretty clumsy with my left, which means that although I'm competent at Continental knitting, I'll never be very fast at it.

Continental knitting can be faster than English, as it's ergonomically more efficient—your hands and yarn are moving less. If you're good at one, it's wise to try the other out to expand your skills, but neither technique is clearly better. Use what works for you.

There is a third method—less common, but popular among "serious" knitters—combination knitting. Annie Modesitt is the acknowledged master of this technique. It's very fast, but it does require a couple of adjustments to patterns to compensate for a slight change in how the stitches are structured. Modesitt has written a fabulous book on this technique: *Confessions of a Knitting Heretic* (or visit http://anniemodesitt.com/combo for more information).

CARE OF KNITWEAR, OR, "I THREW THAT SWEATER YOU KNIT IN THE WASHING MACHINE AND IT WENT FUNNY"

RULE #1: Pay attention to the washing instructions for the yarn on the ball band. If it says "hand wash only" or "do not machine wash" or words to this effect, pay attention. If you're unsure about the mysterious symbols on the yarn label, Wikipedia has an excellent explanation of them all: http://en.wikipedia.org/wiki/Laundry_symbol.

Wool needs to be specially treated to be machine-washable—also known as "superwash" wool. If it doesn't say superwash, it's likely to felt when you wash it. "Felting" is what happens to wool when you subject it to agitation and heat. The scales on the wool fibers stand up and act like Velcro, causing the fabric to thicken and shrink. An accidentally felted sweater will emerge smaller than when you knit it and will have lost all its stretch. Felted knitting is a terrific fabric for bags and pillows and the like, but lousy for garments.

RULE #2: If in doubt, hand wash. A good wool wash like Soak™ or Eucalan™ is best for this purpose, as they don't require rinsing out. Use the quantity indicated, and let the items soak for the required time—usually about 15 minutes. Gently squeeze the water out and roll the items in a towel to pull some of the water out. Do not twist or wring the items. Lay flat to dry.

> ### DIRTY SECRET
>
> *Handwashing is actually better for your garments than dry-cleaning, particularly if they are wool or another animal fiber. The solvents used in dry-cleaning take the natural oils out of the fiber, shortening their lifespan.*

Improperly washed wool shrinks and felts.

This is another good reason to swatch, by the way: you can test to see if the yarn will withstand a machine wash! If the ball band says the yarn is machine washable, I will give it a gentle spin in my washing machine to get most of the water out.

RULE #3: Treat your knitting as gently as you are able. If it's a machine-washable wool and you're putting it in the machine, I recommend a gentle cycle with a gentle detergent/wash. I also don't put like to put my hand knits in the dryer. Using an automatic clothes dryer can encourage shrinking and fading and general wear and tear on your woolies.

RULE #4: No coat hangers. Items should be folded and stored flat. Hanging garments can cause them to stretch.

RULE #5: If you're packing items away for any length of time, wash them first and pack them into airtight bags with cedar balls to discourage moths.

GOOD REFERENCES: WHERE TO GO NEXT

Vogue Knitting: The Ultimate Knitting Book is the best all-around reference book for knitters looking to expand their skills. It goes deep on a wide range of topics, and it's reasonably easy. Although a little less beginner friendly, Montse Stanley's *Reader's Digest Knitting Handbook* is a masterwork, and will support you through your entire knitting career.

Knittinghelp.com and Knitty.com both have extensive learning material. Knitty.com has many articles on a broad range of topics and skills. Knittinghelp.com has videos of all the key techniques and stitches, which can be a great help when learning.

In addition, knittinghelp.com has editorial text to accompany the videos, helping to explain not only how to do something, but why. The Increases and Decreases pages alone are invaluable: for every increase and decrease demonstrated in a video, they have clear pictures of the result, and notes on why you might choose one over the other.

Although there are a lot of knitting videos on youtube.com and other video websites, I find that they are not of consistent quality—some are tremendously good, others not so much.

Yarnstandards.com is a terrific resource maintained by the Craft Yarn Council of America. It has a wealth of reference information, including tables of needle sizes, yarn gauge information, sizing standards, and so forth.

Yarndex.com is a remarkably well-maintained site that provides information about commercially available yarns—providing gauge info, fiber content, care instructions, color names and codes, and even availability information. It's not complete, but it's got a huge number of yarns listed.

All subsequent chapters will point you to good books on that specific topic.

GOOD SOURCES FOR FREE PATTERNS

Knitty.com is the venerable grand dame of online knitting sites—it has hundreds of wonderful free patterns, and every last one of them has been proofread and edited for ease of knitting and reading.

Bernat.com, berroco.com, lionbrand.com and patonsyarns.com all have extensive collections of free patterns; although, of course, they are written for their own brands of yarn, there's sufficient yarn information on the websites to help you make substitutions. Some of these sites may require you to set up a free account—they want your email address so that they can send you email newsletters. Let them—the newsletters often have free patterns, too. And you can feel comfortable that these patterns have been through the eyes of a technical editor. A lot of the smaller yarn companies have free patterns, too. The collections might not be as big, but their designs are just as wonderful—if not a little more! I love the patterns that spudandchloe.com offer, for example.

Many of the knitting magazines have websites with free patterns, too. Vogueknitting.com, creativeknittingmagazine.com and interweaveknits.com all offer up popular patterns from back issues, and sometimes specially featured patterns from new and upcoming issues. As with the yarn company sites, the newsletters often have free patterns. The magazine websites also often have additional photographs of the garments, and sometimes will show you what they look like on different models, to help you get a better sense of how a garment really looks.

Chapter 6: Shaping

INTRODUCTION

Shaping—by which we mean increasing and decreasing—is the key to moving beyond scarves and squares in your knitting. Increasing and decreasing means that you can make pieces wider, or narrow, or round, or triangular. Shaping opens up your world to include sweaters, has, mittens, socks, toys, and beyond.

DECREASES

K2TOG & P2TOG

You've probably encountered a decrease already: the most common is k2tog—knit two stitches together. It's as straightforward as it sounds. Its counterpart on the purl side is p2tog.

SKILLS TAUGHT

DECREASING: K2tog, k2tog tbl, SKP, SSK, p2tog, k3tog, p3tog, SSSK, S2KPO, SK2PO.

INCREASING: Kfb, M1F, M1B, backwards loop M1, left and right lifted increases, yo.

OTHER SKILLS: Use of markers and stitch holders, measuring gauge in garter stitch, blocking, rejoining yarn to stitches, mattress stitch, one-piece garment construction.

Decrease swatch, knit side: from top to bottom, k2tog, ssk, skp, k2tog tbl, s2kpo, sk2po

Decrease swatch, purl side: from top to bottom, p2tog, p3tog

These decreases take two stitches and make one. Both decreases lean to the right. You can see this clearly with the k2tog in the photo below.

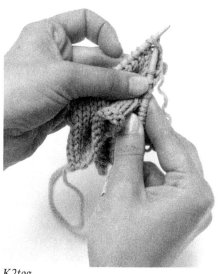

K2tog

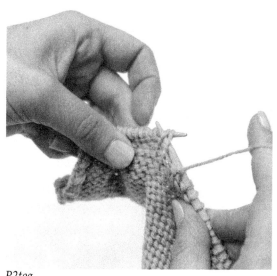

P2tog

K2TOG TBL, SKP, AND SSK

These three decreases are very closely related—they all do what k2tog does in that they take two stitches and make them into one. But these three decreases all lean to the left. Why left-leaning? The direction a decrease leans doesn't matter in every application, but in some, like waist shaping on a sweater, and lace, it looks much better.

Using a left-leaning decrease on the right side of a piece makes for a much neater line than if you were to use a right-leaning decrease.

Why are there three versions of a left-leaning decrease? Each looks slightly different—the stitches are angled differently. It's a minor detail, and in the vast majority of cases you should just use the one you find easiest! It only really matters in lace knitting, and even then, it's not that big a deal. A designer will specify the one he or she likes best, but if you prefer a different version, substitute your favorite, guilt-free.

K2tog tbl—knit 2 together through the back loop. That is, the needle point goes into the loop that is on the back of your needle, through the two stitches.

SKP stands for slip 1, knit 1, then pass slipped stitch over. It is worked as it sounds: slip the next stitch knitwise—that is, stick the tip of right hand needle into the stitch like you're going to knit it, but just slide it over to the right-hand needle—knit the next stitch normally, and then lift the slipped stitch over the newly knit stitch, just like you're binding off.

SSK—this is the oddest of the three in how it's worked, although it's my personal favorite as it matches k2tog best of all, and therefore looks good when the two are worked close together. Slip two stitches one by one, as if to knit. These two stitches are now on the right-hand needle. Now stick the point of the left needle into the fronts of these two stitches from left to right, wrap the yarn around the point of the right needle as normal, and knit the two stitches together.

There are purl versions of a left-leaning decrease, but they are very rarely used. If a pattern needs such a rare creature, it will be very specific about how to do it.

K3TOG, SSSK, AND P3TOG

These are all double decreases—that is, they take three stitches and reduce them down to one. K3tog and p3tog, worked precisely as they sound, are just more "extreme" versions of k2tog and p2tog. They still lean to the right. And in that vein, you can also do an SSSK, slipping three stitches rather than two—that decrease leans to the left, as you might expect.

S2KPO AND SK2PO

S2KPO and SK2PO are centered double decreases; they neither lean left nor right.

S2KPO is worked as follows: slip the next 2 stitches together, as if to k2tog. Knit the next stitch, then pass the 2 slipped stitches over the stitch just knit.

SK2PO is worked as follows: slip the next stitch; k2tog, then pass the slipped stitch over the k2tog.

The difference between these two is subtle but important—S2KPO creates a strong vertical line, but SK2PO breaks that vertical line. It's a visual difference only—neither decrease leans, it's all about how they look.

K2togtbl

SKP

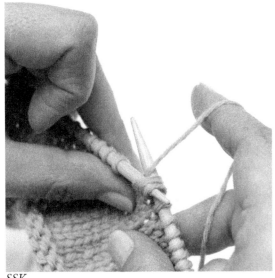

SSK

As with the left-leaning decreases, which you use is really a matter of preference. I prefer S2KPO myself, as it looks tidier, but it's your choice.

DECREASES IN PATTERNS

In most situations, the pattern will be very specific about the decrease required, e.g.: *Row 1: K2tog, k to last 2 sts, ssk.*

If the decrease isn't specified, the pattern will at least tell you how many stitches to decrease, e.g.: *Decrease 1 stitch at the start of the following row.* If you're on a knit row, you won't go wrong with k2tog, if you're on a purl row, use p2tog. If the instruction asks more (e.g. *Decrease 1 stitch at each end of the following row*) it's time to get fancy. This is precisely the situation with the swatch photographed at left. To create clean lines, it's a good idea to use paired decreases: a left-leaning on one side, and a right-leaning on the other. I usually work an ssk at the start of the row and a k2tog at the end. And since a decrease at the very start or end of a row makes your edges wobbly, I work them 1 stitch in from the edges, to keep everything tidy (and to make it easier for sewing up or adding an edging), as follows: *K1, ssk, k to last 3 sts, k2tog, k1.*

INCREASES

These are all single increases, adding one stitch.

KFB

This is often the first increase a knitter learns: knit through the front and back of the stitch. To do this, knit into the front of the stitch as normal, but don't slip it off your left-hand needle. Swing the tip of the right-hand needle around to the back loop of the stitch still on your left needle and knit it again, then slip both stitches off your left needle.

It's easy and effective, but not very pretty. The "b" portion creates a little bump like a purl stitch. I only use it when I'm increasing in or immediately after ribbing, as it hides nicely.

S2KPO, SK2PO

Decreases in patterns: using an ssk on the right side and a k2tog on the left side makes a cleaner line (bottom section of swatch). Using a k2tog on both sides changes how the piece lies (top section of swatch).

Increases: KFB, M1Z, M1R, M1L, yo, left and right lifted increases

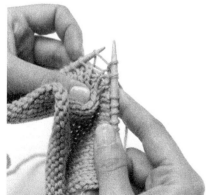

KFB step 1

KFB step 2

KFB step 3

M1Z

THE M1 FAMILY

"M1" stands for "make 1," by which we mean to make a stitch where there wasn't one before. There are a number of ways to do this. My personal favorite is what I've come to call **M1Z**, after Elizabeth Zimmermann, who popularized the technique: simply make a backwards loop (as in the backwards loop cast on), and place it on your right-hand needle.

I love this increase because it's neutral: it doesn't have a particular lean, and it doesn't favor knit or purl. It will be whatever you need it to be.

Left-leaning M1 (also known as M1L or M1F): Put the tip of the left-hand needle from *front to back* under the bar between the first stitch on the left needle and the last stitch on the right needle. Knit this bar through the *back* loop.

Right-leaning M1 (also known as M1R or M1B): Put the tip of the left-hand needle from *back to front* under the bar between the first stitch on the left needle and the last stitch on the right needle. Knit this bar through the *front* loop.

M1L step 1

M1L step 2

M1R step 1

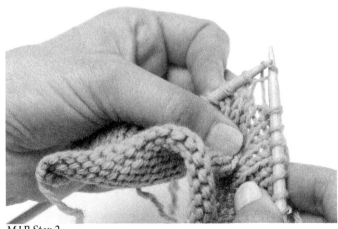

M1R Step 2

These two can be a bit trickier to work, although the biggest challenge for me is remembering which leans left and which leans right (and truth be told, if you mix them up it's not the end of the world).

YARNOVER

The yarnover is a decorative increase—that is, it's very visible. On the knit side, bring the yarn to the front between the points of the needles, as if you were going to purl, and then keep working. The yarn wraps itself over the needle, and creates a loop that becomes a new stitch when worked on the next row. Note that the yarnover itself is the full stitch. The following knit or purl stitch is its own stitch. On the purl side, wrap the yarn over the top of the needle and back around to the front. The yarnover is the basis of lace knitting and, used in the right situation, is a wonderful thing. Just don't use it when you need an invisible increase or when you don't want holes in your fabric.

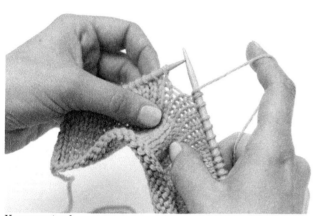

Yarnover step 1

Yarnover step 2

LIFTED INCREASES

LLI: Use the left needle to pick up the left side of the stitch two below the stitch just knitted, then knit into it.
RLI: Use the right needle to pick up the right side of the stitch below the about-to-be-worked stitch on the left needle. Place it on the left needle, then knit into it.

These both qualify as "make 1" in that they make stitches out of nothing. The only downside to these two is that you can't do a lot of them in close proximity, as they can pucker your work. I also struggle a bit to remember which leans left and which leans right.

INCREASES IN PATTERNS

It's fairly common in patterns that the designer isn't specific about which increase they wish you to use, e.g. *Increase 1 st at each end of this row.* The designer might ask for an M1 without telling you which kind. This lets you know that it doesn't really matter which you use, as long as you end up with the right number of stitches at the end of the row. I will choose the M1Z most often.

As with decreases, it generally looks better if you place them one stitch in from the edge, e.g.: *K1, M1Z, k to last st, M1Z, k1.*

And if I choose to use directional increases, I'll place the right-leaning one at the start of the row, and the left-leaning on at the end, e.g.: *K1, M1F, k to last st, M1B, k1.*

KFB is tricky in this situation, as it makes a visible bump to the left of the stitch on which you work it, so to place the increases one stitch in from the edge, you would work as follows: *KFB, k to 2 sts before the end, KFB, k1.* KFB can also be problematic because it "uses up" a stitch to make the increase. You need to be careful about the counting if you're working a number of increases in a row. For example, consider a situation where you have a row of 60 stitches and you need to add 5 stitches. If you work 5 M1s, the other 60 stitches are knitted normally. If you use 5 KFBs, then only 55 stitches are worked normally; five of them are worked for the KFBs.

Sometimes, you'll see the phrasing "increase 1 in the next stitch"—KFB is the right choice in this situation.

MINI PROJECT: DIAMOND GARTER STITCH DISHCLOTH

This project allows you to practice a lot of different skills very quickly. Even if it doesn't work out perfectly the first time, it will still be a very usable dishcloth.

Special stitches used: yarnover, ssk, k2tog, s2kpo.
Other skills: measuring gauge in garter stitch.

FINISHED MEASUREMENTS
Approximately 8 inches/20 cm square.

MATERIALS
1 50gm ball Sugar & Cream Cotton (100% cotton, 120 yds/2.5 oz ball)—sample uses color #00004, ecru.
4.5mm (US #7) needles
A safety pin

GAUGE
18 sts and 17 ridges = 4 ins by 4 ins/10 cm by 10 cm in garter stitch
You don't need to check your gauge before you start, but partway through the project you should check to make sure you're getting something close. Note that when measuring gauge in garter stitch, it's almost impossible to count individual rows, so we measure ridges instead. A ridge is 2 rows.

METHOD
When working this pattern, check off the rows as you go. There's lots going on, and if you're not sure what row you're on, it can be challenging.

Cast on 3 sts.
Increase section:
Row 1 [RS]: KFB twice, k1. 5 sts.
Row 2 [WS]: Knit.
Row 3: K2, yo, k1, yo, k2. 7 sts. Place a safety pin at the start of this row. You'll use this to keep track of which row is which.
Row 4 [WS]: Knit.
Row 5 [RS]: K2, yo, k to last 2 sts, yo, k2. 2 sts increased.
Row 6 [WS]: Knit.
Repeat the last 2 rows until you have 45 stitches, ending after a plain Knit row.

Decrease section:
Row 1 [RS]: K2, yo, ssk twice, k to last 6 sts, k2tog twice, yo, k2. 2 sts decreased.
Note: You have to decrease twice on each side here to both compensate for the yo increase and also decrease the total number of stitches.
Row 2 [WS]: Knit.
Repeat the last 2 rows until you have 11 stitches, ending after a plain Knit row.

Final decreases:
Row 1 [RS]: K2, yo, ssk, s2kpo, k2tog, yo, k2. 9 sts.
Row 2 [WS]: K3, s2kpo, k3. 7 sts.
Row 3 [RS]: K2, yo, s2kpo, yo, k2. 7 sts.
Row 4 [WS]: K2, s2kpo, k2. 5 sts.
Row 5 [RS]: K1, s2kpo, k1. 3 sts.
Bind off.
Finishing:
Weave in ends.

At left: Bias Knit Scarf (pattern begins page 47)

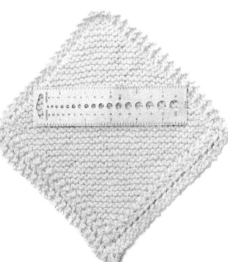

To check your stitch gauge, measure 4 inches horizontally and count the bumps of the stitches.

To check your row gauge, measure 2 inches vertically and count the ridges.

BIAS KNIT SCARF

(As pictured on page 44.) A great use for all those gorgeous hand-dyed skeins of luxury yarn, this scarf is worked on the bias. In straight rows a variegated yarn gives stripes, and the construction here tips those stripes on an angle. This simple change makes all the difference in the world to how the finished scarf looks and wears.

Special stitches used: M1Z, k2tog.
Other skills: using a larger needle for binding off.

FINISHED MEASUREMENTS
Approximately 62 inches /157 cm long x 4 inches/10 cm wide after blocking.

MATERIALS
1 100gm skein Schaefer Helene (50% merino wool, 50% cultivated silk, 218 yds/100gm skein)—sample uses color Aung San Suu Kyi
You can also substitute about 200–250yds of any luxurious yarn in a worsted or Aran weight—Malabrigo Worsted, Twist or Rios would work wonderfully.

5mm (US #8) needles, straight or short circular, as you prefer
safety pin or removable stitch marker
a single 6mm (US #10) needle for binding off

GAUGE
As with the dishcloth, it's not critical to match gauge here, as long as you like the fabric that results. Do a quick check after you've worked an inch or two to make sure you're close.
17 sts and 21 ridges = 4 ins by 4 ins/10 cm by 10 cm in garter stitch

METHOD
Cast on 36 stitches.
Row 1 [RS]: K1, M1Z, k to last 2 sts, k2tog.
Row 2 [WS]: Knit.
Repeat these 2 rows until you've almost run out of yarn, ending with a WS row.

Tip: put a safety pin or removable stitch marker in the fabric at the start of the RS row. It helps you keep track of which row you're on.

Bind off loosely, using the larger needle in your right hand.

Finishing
Weave in ends.

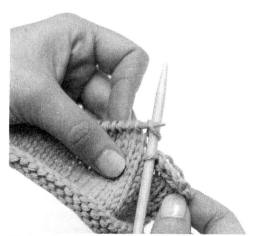

Binding off with a larger needle.

TOP-DOWN TRIANGLE SHAWL

(As pictured on facing page.) Special stitches used: KFB.
Other skills: Use of markers, intro to blocking.

FINISHED MEASUREMENTS
In Socks That Rock: *(seen on page 46)* Approximately 44 inches/112cm wide x 18 inches/46 cm long after blocking.
In Rowan Felted Tweed *(seen on page 38)*: Approximately 54 inches/137 cm wide x 21 inches/54 cm long after blocking.

MATERIALS
1 155gm skein Socks that Rock Mediumweight (100% Merino, 380yd/skein). Sample uses color Gertrude Skein.
3.5mm (US #4) needles— a 24 inch/60 cm circular is easiest, but you can use straight needles if you prefer
a single 5mm (US #8) needle for binding off
a stitch marker

OR
2 x 50gm balls Rowan Felted Tweed (50% Merino, 25% Alpaca, 25% Viscose, 190yds/175m per 50gm ball). Sample uses color 150.
4.5mm needles (US #7)—a 24 inch/60 cm circular is easiest, but you can use straight needles if you prefer
a single 6mm (US #10) needle for binding off
a stitch marker

You can also substitute approximately 380yds/350m of any sport or double knitting weight yarn—a little more yarn will make a larger shawl; a little less yarn will make a smaller shawl. Use needles a size or two larger than recommended for your chosen yarn, to make a nice drapey fabric.

GAUGE
In Socks That Rock: approximately 21 sts and 34 rows = 4 ins by 4 ins/10 cm by 10 cm in stockinette stitch.
In Rowan Felted Tweed: approximately 16 sts and 26 rows = 4 ins by 4 ins/10 cm by 10 cm in stockinette stitch.

It's not critical for this project—what's most important is that you like how the fabric looks and feels. After you've work a couple of inches, take a good look at what you've knitted. If you like how it looks—not too floppy or loose, not too stiff—keep going. If not, change needles and start again. If it's too floppy, go down a couple of needle sizes; if it's too tight, go up a couple of needle sizes.

METHOD
Top Edge
The top edge is established in garter stitch.

Using your favorite method, cast on 9 sts.
Row 1 [RS]: KFB, k2, KFB twice, k2, KFB, k1. 13 sts.
Row 2 [WS]: Knit.
Row 3 [RS]: KFB, k4, KFB twice, k4, KFB, k1. 17 sts.
Row 4 [WS]: Knit.
Row 5 [RS]: KFB, k6, KFB twice, k6, KFB, k1. 21 sts.
Row 6 [WS]: K11, place marker on the right-hand needle, k10.

Body
The body is worked in an 8-row pattern. On each RS row, 4 increases are worked—one at each end, and two in the middle. The placement of the increases is what makes the shape—the increases in the middle push the rows out sideways, on an angle. The marker helps you keep track of where to do those increases.

Row 1 [RS]: K3, KFB, k to 1 st before center marker, KFB, slip marker, KFB, k until 5 sts rem, KFB, k4.
Row 2 [WS]: K4, p to last 4 sts, k4.
Row 3 [RS]: K3, KFB, k to 1 st before center marker, KFB, slip marker, KFB, k until 5 sts rem, KFB, k4.
Row 4 [WS]: K4, p to last 4 sts, k4.
Row 5 [RS]: K3, KFB, k to 1 st before center marker, KFB, slip marker, KFB, k until 5 sts rem, KFB, k4.
Row 6 [WS]: K4, p to last 4 sts, k4.
Row 7 [RS]: K3, KFB, k to 1 st before center marker, KFB, slip marker, KFB, k until 5 sts rem, KFB, k4.
Row 8 [WS]: K all sts.

Repeat the above 8 rows until you're almost out of yarn, ending after a Row 8.

Lower Edge
You'll work a few rows of garter stitch and then bind off.
Ensure RS is facing. Knit 5 rows. WS will be facing. Using the larger needle in your right hand, bind off knitwise.

Finishing
Soak the finished shawl in lukewarm water for 10 or 15 minutes. Roll in a towel or if the yarn is machine washable, run through the spin cycle of your washing machine to wring it out. Stretch it out and pin the three corners to your laundry rack, or a mattress, or blocking mats, or towels on the floor and leave to air dry.

KNITTERLY ADVICE

Experienced knitters don't make fewer mistakes. In fact, they often make bigger mistakes. But experienced knitters know how to fix them, and — most importantly — not to beat themselves up over them. Mistakes happen. It's part of knitting.

— Amy R. Singer, knitty.com

ONE-PIECE BABY SWEATER

Other skills: Use of stitch holders, rejoining yarn to stitches, mattress stitch, one-piece garment construction.

Don't be intimidated by the length of these instructions—it's pretty quick and easy knitting. I've simply explained it in lots of detail. This is a classic top-down, one-piece sweater. It starts at the collar. You divide the row up into five sections—left front, left sleeve, back, right sleeve, and right front. The four dividing lines between these points are the raglan lines—and increases are worked at these points to build the yoke of the sweater.

Top-down garments are popular because they are easy and require minimal finishing—very few seams to sew up. You can length or shorten them to suit the wearer—or the available yarn—just knit the body (and sleeves as required) for more or less distance than the pattern calls for. Top-down construction is also rewarding because you see the garment taking shape quickly, and it's easy to visualize what you're doing. Even if you don't have a baby to knit for, this is a great introduction to knitting garments. Make the sweater and donate it to a local charity or women's shelter.

SIZES and FINISHED MEASUREMENTS

Size	Finished Chest	Body Length	Sleeve Length
Preemie–newborn	16.75 inches/42 cm	8 inches/20 cm	7 inches/ 17.5 cm
3 months	18.5 inches/46 cm	10 inches/25 cm	7.5 inches/19 cm
6 months	20 inches/50 cm	11 inches/27.5 cm	8 inches/ 20 cm
12 months	21.5 inches/54 cm	12 inches/30 cm	8.5 inches/ 21 cm
18 months	23.25 inches/ 58 cm	13 inches/32.5 cm	9 inches/ 22.5cm

MATERIALS
3 (4, 5, 5, 5) 50gm balls KnitPicks Comfy Worsted (75% pima cotton, 25% acrylic, 109 yds/50 gm ball). Sample uses color Serrano.
4.5mm needles —a 24 inch/60 cm circular is easiest, but you can use straight needles if you prefer
two lengths of smooth scrap yarn or unwaxed dental floss
a darning needle
a single 6mm needle for binding off
8 stitch markers
1 ½-inch button

GAUGE
20 sts and 28 rows = 4 ins by 4 ins/10 cm by 10 cm in stockinette stitch using 4.5mm needles.
Unlike the other projects in this section, gauge does matter. You need to knit to gauge to make sure that the sweater will turn out to be the right size. Refer to page 19 for information on how to check gauge.

METHOD

Numbers for the smallest size are first; numbers for larger sizes follow afterwards in brackets. Where there in only one number, it applies to all sizes.

Collar

Cast on 48 (48, 56, 56, 56) stitches.

Knit every row until piece measures 2.5 (2.75, 3, 3.25, 3.5) inches from cast on edge.

Yoke

Next row, set up markers for increases (WS): K7 (7, 8, 8, 8), place a marker on your right-hand needle, k1, place a second marker on your right-hand needle; k8 (8, 10, 10, 10). Place a third marker on your right-hand needle, k1, place a fourth marker on your right-hand needle. K14 (14, 16, 16, 16). Place a fifth marker on your right-hand needle, k1, place a sixth marker on your right-hand needle. K8 (8, 10, 10, 10). Place a seventh marker on your right-hand marker, k1, place an eighth marker on your right-hand needle. K7 (7, 8, 8, 8) to end of row.

The 7 (7, 8, 8, 8)stitches at the start and end of the row will form the fronts of the sweater; the 14 (14, 16, 16, 16) stitches in the middle will be the back; the groups of 10 (10, 12, 12, 12) stitches (including the marked stitches) are the sleeves. You've got four marked stitches—that is, four stitches that have a marker on each side. You'll be working increases on each side of these 4 marked stitches on every RS row.

Row 1, increase row (RS): K to first marker, m1f, slip marker to right-hand needle, k1, slip next marker to right hand needle, m1b. K to third marker, m1f, slip marker to right-hand needle, k1, slip next marker to right-hand needle, m1b. K to fifth marker, m1f, slip marker to right-hand needle, k1, slip next marker to right-hand needle, m1b. K to seventh marker, m1f, slip marker to right-hand needle, k1, slip next marker to right hand needle, m1b. K to end. 8 stitches increased—one each side of all four marked stitches.

Row 2 (WS): K4, p to last 4 sts, k4.

The rest of the garment is working in stockinette stitch with a garter stitch edging: RS rows are knitted all the way across, with increases. Wrong side rows have 4 knit stitches at each end to form the edging, and the rest of the stitches are purled.

Repeat the last 2 rows twice more.

Next increase row, work a buttonhole as follows: K to first marker, m1f, slip marker to right-hand needle, k1, slip next marker to right-hand needle, m1b. K to third marker, m1f, slip marker to right-hand needle, k1, slip next marker to right-hand needle, m1b. K to fifth marker, m1f, slip marker to right-hand needle, k1, slip next marker to right-hand needle, m1b. K to seventh marker, m1f, slip marker to right-hand needle, k1, slip next marker to right-hand needle, m1b. K to last 4 sts, k2tog, yo, k2.

Following row (WS): K4, p to last 4 sts, k4.

Now go back and work Rows 1 & 2 again, repeating them 9 (11, 12, 14, 16) more times.

You should have 152 (168, 184, 200, 216) stitches total. 20 (22, 24, 26, 28) sts each for the two fronts, 40 (44, 48, 52, 56) sts for back and 36 (40, 44, 48, 52) sts each for the two sleeves (including the marked stitches). If you're off by a stitch or two in either direction, don't worry. If you're short more than 3 or 4 stitches, keep working the 2-row pattern until you're close.

Measure the piece from the bottom of the collar. You need it to be about 3.75 (4.25, 4.5, 5, 5.75) inches from the bottom of the collar. If it's close or a little bit over, move to the next step, dividing up body and sleeves.

If it's too short, work as follows:

RS row: Knit.

WS row: K4, p to last 4 st, k4.

Repeat these two rows until piece measures this distance, ending with a WS row. If it's a little bit over or under that measurement, it's ok.

Mattress stitch step 1

Mattress stitch step2

Pull the seaming yarn to close up the seam

Divide up Body and Sleeves
Have your darning needle and scrap yarn ready. At this point, you'll set the sleeve stitches aside, and continue work on the body stitches only.

Dividing row (RS): K56 (62, 68, 74, 80) removing markers as you go. Thread the last 36 (40, 44, 48, 52) sts just knit onto your scrap yarn/dental floss. These stitches will form the first sleeve. Tie the ends of the scrap yarn together to keep the stitches secure. K40 (44, 48, 52, 56) sts of back and the 36 (40, 44, 48, 52) sts of the second sleeve, removing markers as you go. As before, thread the 36 (40, 44, 48, 52) sts just knit to a length of scrap yarn/dental floss. K to end of row. 80 (88, 96, 104, 112) sts on the needle for the body; two sets of 36 (40, 44, 48, 52) sts on hold for the sleeves.
Following row (WS): K4, purl to first gap, cast on two stitches using the M1Z, p to next gap, cast on 2 sts as before, p to last 4 sts, k4. 84 (92, 100, 108, 116) sts total.

Body row 1 (RS): Knit.
Body row 2 (WS): K4, p to last 4 sts, k4.
Repeat the last two rows until piece measures 3.25 (4.75, 5.5, 6, 6.25) inches from dividing point, ending with a WS row.

Lower edging row 1 (RS): Knit.
Lower edging row 2 (WS): Knit.
Repeat these two rows twice more, and then row 1 once more. You should have 3 garter ridges. Bind off, using the larger needle. Leave yourself a 5 or 6 inch tail.

Sleeves
Return the 36 (40, 44, 48, 52) sts of the first sleeve to your needle. With RS facing—that is, as the start of the row when you're looking at the knit side—rejoin yarn, and knit across all the stitches. Using the M1Z, cast on 1 st at the end of the row. 37 (41, 45, 49, 53) sts.
Row 2 (WS): P to end, and again cast on 1 st at the end of the row. 38 (42, 46, 50, 54) sts.
Row 3 (RS): Knit.
Row 4 (WS): Purl.

Decrease row (RS): K1, ssk, k to last 3 sts, k2tog, k1. 2 sts decreased.
Work 11 (9, 7, 9, 7) rows even in stockinette stitch, starting with a WS row.

Repeat that 12 (10, 8, 10, 8) row pattern 2 (3, 4, 4, 5) more times.
Work one more decrease row. 30 (32, 34, 38, 40) sts.

QUICK TIP

How to work mattress stitch:

If you stretch out your knitting sideways, you'll see that in the center of each knit stitch there is a bar. You'll use these bars for the seaming.

Line up the sleeves, with right sides facing. (Yes, that's right, you seam knitting with the right sides facing). You can optionally pin the two pieces together with a few safety pins to act as milestones as you go. Thread your yarn tail from the cast-off onto your darning needle. Seam as follows: grab a bar on one side, in the center of the first stitch on the edge. Grab a bar on the second side, immediately across from the first. Repeat, picking up every bar, alternating sides. Pull snug as you work.

Work even—no decreases—until sleeve measures approximately 6 (6.5, 7. 7.5, 8) inches from dividing point, ending with a WS row. If it's a little longer, it's ok.

Lower edging row 1 (RS): Knit.

Lower edging row 2 (WS): Knit.

Repeat these two rows twice more, and then row 1 once more. You should have 3 garter ridges. Bind off, using the larger needle, and leave yourself a 12 inch long tail.

Repeat this for the second sleeve.

FINISHING

Sew sleeves using mattress stitch—see above. Sew cast-on stitches at underarm together—turn garment inside out and backstitch or whip-stitch. Weave in ends. Sew on button to left side to match buttonhole. Wash.

KNITTERLY ADVICE

When counting stitches, hold the pointy end of the needle and start counting there. If you count from the other end, it's too easy to knock stitches off the needle.

— Maryjean Lancefield, knitter

The arrows mark the raglan increase lines on the baby sweater (there are corresponding lines on the back of the sweater, too).

Chapter 7: In the Round

INTRODUCTION

Hats, mittens, and socks: all are projects that are better and more easily knitted in the round. Working in the round allows you to create circles and tubes without having to sew seams later. In the case of hats and mittens, it's a great time saver. In the case of socks, it's essential: a sock with a seam is uncomfortable to wear.

And, rather remarkably, working in the round is easier because there's significantly less purling! To work in the round, you need either double-pointed needles or a circular needle.

SKILLS TAUGHT

Working in the round: on double pointed and circular needles.

OTHER SKILLS: Long-tail cast on, slipping stitches, binding off in ribbing.

WHY TWO TYPES OF NEEDLES?

There are two types of needles for working in the round: double-pointed needles (which come in sets of four or five), and circular needles, which are flexible cords with needles at both ends. The process with either needle type is the same—it's all about circumference. When working with a circular needle, you are limited by the length of the needle. When working on circular needles, the circumference of the piece you are working must be larger than the length of the needle, so that the stitches can fit comfortably around. The smallest commonly available length of circular needle is 16 inches (40 cm), and so if you're working a piece smaller—a mitten or a sock, for example—you need to work with double-pointed needles.

HOW TO GET STARTED

To work in the round you cast on as you would normally, onto one needle. For practice purposes, use whichever cast on you like best, but for most in-the-round patterns, you need a good stretchy cast on. For these projects I like the long-tail cast on. It creates a nice, low-profile edge With this cast on, you have complete control over how tight or loose an edge you are creating, so ensure that you're keeping a bit of room between the stitches on the needle—don't pull it super tight.

Make a slip knot a reasonable distance★ up the yarn. Put the slip knot on your needle and hold it in your right hand, using your index finger to hold the slip knot in place.

With your left hand, make a fist around the two strands of yarn and pull them down so that they are taut. With your thumb and forefinger pointing towards the wrist of your right hand, separate the two strands.

★What's "a reasonable distance"? That is, how long a tail do you actually need? You'll never run short if you leave 1 inch per stitch. You'll have too much, but you'll never run short. There are more accurate ways of estimating, but I prefer a longer tail so that I can use it to sew up if required. You do use the two strands up at different rates, and if you get them reversed and haven't left yourself a generous enough tail, you risk running out of yarn. The short end should be over your thumb; the ball end over your finger.

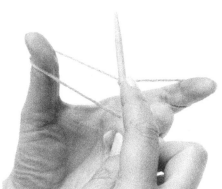

Tilt your palm up so that the thumb and forefinger are pointing up and the needle is resting between them.

Using your right hand, move the point of the needle over top of the far strand on your thumb to grab it.

Then swing the needle to the other side and over the top of the near strand of yarn around your finger, grabbing that strand.

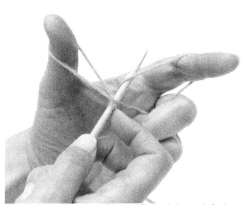

Finally, bring the point of the needle back through the loop on your thumb....

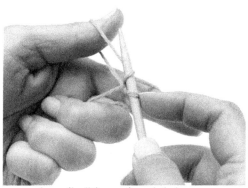

… pass the needle all the way through the loop …

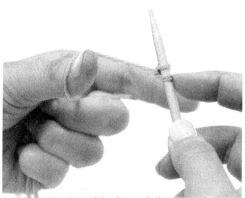

...and a stitch is formed that's stretchy but not too loose. Don't pull the yarn too tight – leave a bit of room between the stitches on your needle.

Once the stitches are all cast on, distribute them appropriately. On double-pointed needles, divide them up as evenly as possible onto three needles. If the number of stitches you have doesn't divide evenly, get it as close as possible. It is a good idea to have an even number of stitches on each needle (that is, a multiple of 2), it makes counting easier. For example, if you've got 24 stitches and three needles, put 8 on each needle; if you've got 26, put 8 each on two needles and 10 on a third. To move the stitches around, slip them across purlwise, which means with your needle positioned as if to purl. If you're working on a circular needle, just make sure you have enough stitches to go comfortably around.

Distributing stitches

JOINING

Patterns for working in the round always start with a sort of terrifying admonition: "join, being careful not to twist," without really explaining how to do it, or what it means.

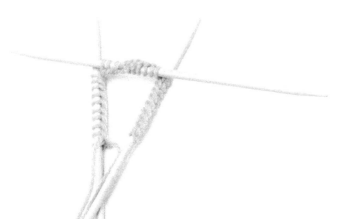

The short explanation is that if you join the stitches with a twist in them, your knitting will end up with a twist in it and will, ultimately, be impossible to knit. A twist in your knitting is unfixable, unfortunately, so it is true that you need to take care that it doesn't happen. The good news is that it's easy to recognize and prevent. After the cast on but before you join the edges to begin knitting in the round, make sure all the stitches are facing the same direction: lay the needle(s) down in a "circular" shape, and ensure all the bumps of the stitches are in the middle, and that there aren't any stitches running over a needle (see picture at left, a round with a twist in it).

A round with a twist in it

To join the round, identify the stitch with the working yarn hanging from it, and then identify the stitch at the far other end—the first stitch you cast on. Using the unused needle from your set, knit that first cast-on stitch with the working yarn. This pulls the first and last stitches of the round close together, and joins the round.

When working in the round—no matter what needle configuration you choose— you're only actually knitting with two needles at a time, just as if you were knitting straight. The other two or three needles sit in the back, essentially serving as very annoying stitch holders. The first few rounds are challenging—it's like riding a bicycle: until you have some momentum, it's a bit wobbly. Everyone develops their own method for holding the needles; it does feel a bit like a porcupine at first. I like to hold my needles so that the two I'm working with are close to me, and the other two are in the back. This way, I'm facing the right side (outside) of the knitting, and it grows downwards.

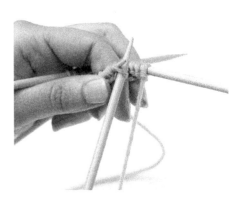

Working the first stitch of the round

Working the first stitch of the round, step 2

And here's a dirty secret: if the round is twisted, you *do* have a chance to fix it, but only after you've knitted your first round. This is the only post-cast-on chance you will have, but it can save you some serious trouble and effort. After the first round has been worked, check again to see if the round is twisted. If it is, you can untwist it at this point—move the stitches around until they're all pointing in the same direction and the twist is in the join. It's sort of a cheat, but it's invisible in the final result. After the second round, check one more time to make sure you're not twisted. All should be well, and you can proceed.

WORKING IN THE ROUND

When working in the round, we don't talk about rows, we talk about rounds. A pattern will give instructions for each round. If you're working on a set of four double-pointed needles, a round is three full needles worth of knitting—all the way back to where you started. You can tell when you're at the start of a round because your two yarns—the working yarn and the cast-on tail—are together again.

If you're working on a circular needle, you need to place a marker before you join so you can keep track of the start of the round.

If you're working on double-pointed needles, and the start of your round is at the start of a needle, you can't place a start of round marker there—it would fall off! Some knitters stick a safety pin (or one of those clever safety-pin-lookalike, removable stitch markers) in the fabric of the knitting, near the start of the round, to help them keep track.

A rather marvelous thing about working in the round is that you don't have to purl. To create stockinette stitch, all you have to do is knit. Recall that to knit stockinette in rows, you knit the right side and purl the wrong side. You don't have to purl when working in the round because you're never working on the wrong side. You're always on the right side (outside) of your knitting, so all you have to do it knit. Although working in the round can seem cumbersome at first, it's absolutely worth it.

QUICK TIP

Slipping stitches:

Slipping a stitch is a simple maneuver—just put the right needle into the stitch and move it from the left needle to the right needle. The key is how to put the needle into the stitch. If you put the needle into the stitch as if you are going to purl—this is known as slipping purlwise. If you put the needle into the stitch as if you are going to knit—this is known as slipping knitwise.

Slipping purlwise preserves the stitch orientation—that is, keeps it the right way on your needle. In general, if the style of the slip not specified, assume you are to slip purlwise.

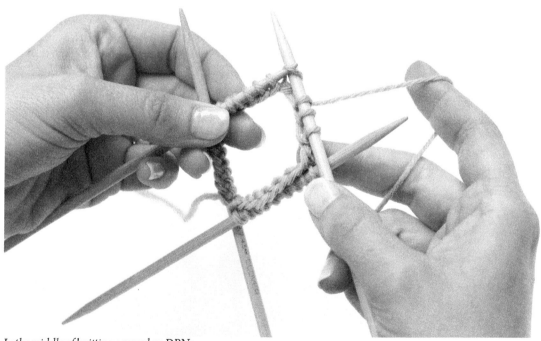

In the middle of knitting a round on DPNs

TROUBLESHOOTING

• When working on double-pointed needles, give the first and last stitch of each needle an extra tug. Looseness between the needles here can lead to unsightly gaps between stitches that knitters call *ladders*.

• You do need to make sure that you're always going around in the right direction: when knitting, the working yarn should always be to your right. Knitting in the round is like walking around the globe—you're always moving forwards, never back: the working yarn hangs off the stitch you've just knit, and you always want to knit the next stitch to the left. If you're about to work into a stitch with the yarn hanging off it, you've turned around and are going in the wrong direction. Keep moving to the left and you'll be fine!

- You can also tell you've turned around if you are suddenly seeing purl stitches on the knit side.
- When working in the round on a set of four dpns, there are always four needles in play—your stitches should be distributed across three needles while you use the fourth to work around. If that fourth one gets forgotten when you're working, you'll end up with your stitches on two needles. Don't worry—just redistribute the stitches again so you're back to the way it was when you started.
- Make sure that the dpns you're using are long enough to comfortably hold all your stitches; if you've got too many on a needle you risk losing some off the ends. In this case, switch to a circular needle (or add another needle, as per the sidebar, page 59).
- Most of these pitfalls can be avoided when working with circular needles, but remember that circular needles don't work in all situations. A hat, for example, can be started at the brim and is therefore large enough to be able to use a circular, but as you decrease to close up the top, you will need to use dpns.

MINI PROJECT: CAT TOY

Other skills: Working in the round on double-pointed needles.

FINISHED MEASUREMENTS
Approximately 2 1/2 inches long.

MATERIALS
1 ball Sirdar Eco Wool (100% undyed virgin wool, 100m per 50gm ball); sample uses color 201 (grey)
1 set 4mm (US #6) double-pointed needles
3.75mm (US #5) double-pointed needles
Safety pin
For stuffing: wool roving or scraps of wool yarn or a scrap of cotton fabric and a teaspoon or so of dried catnip (optional)

GAUGE
Approximately 23 sts and 28 rows = 4 ins by 4 ins/10 cm by 10 cm in stockinette stitch . Gauge doesn't really matter here—a thicker yarn will make a bigger mouse. Two things to note if you are substituting yarn—cats don't like the smell of plastic, so a 100% wool yarn is best, and no matter what yarn you're using, use needles one size smaller than recommended on the ball band—you want to knit a little tighter so the stuffing stays in.

METHOD:
Cast on 12 sts using your favorite method, leaving an 8-inch tail.
Distribute across 3 double-pointed needles - 4 sts on each. Join for working in the round, being careful not to twist.

Knit 1 round even, pulling the first stitch nice and snug. Place a safety pin in the fabric to mark the start of round.
Round 2: (K1, m1, k2, m1, k1) 3 times. 18 sts.
Round 3: Knit.
Round 4: (K1, m1, k4, m1, k1) 3 times. 24 sts.
Rounds 5-9: Knit.
Round 10: (K2tog, k6) 3 times. 21 sts.
Round 11: Knit.

Round 12: (K2tog, k5) 3 times. 18 sts.
Round 13: Knit.
Round 14: (K2tog, k4) 3 times. 15 sts.
Round 15: Knit.
Round 16: (K2tog, k3) 3 times. 12 sts.
Round 17: Knit.
Round 18: (K2tog, k2) 3 times. 9 sts.
Round 19: Knit.
Round 20: (K2tog, k1) 3 times. 6 sts.

Cut yarn, leaving a 4-inch tail. Thread yarn onto darning needle and pull through rem stitches. Cinch to close.

Stuff mouse firmly with a combination of wool roving or snipped wool yarn ends, with a little bundle of catnip wrapped in a tissue in the middle.

Thread tail from cast on onto darning needle and use it to gather the cast-on edge. It doesn't need to be pretty. Pull it tight to close and weave in both ends.

To make a tail, cut three 16 inch lengths of your yarn. Thread them through the gathered cast-on end, ensuring they are hanging evenly - you want 6 threads of about the same length. Tie an overhand knot in all six as close to the top as possible, and then braid the tail together, doubling each strand. When tail is about 5 inches long, finish with another overhand knot, and trim, leaving a 1-inch tassel.

SLOUCHY HAT

Special stitches used: S2kpo
Other skills: Changing from circular to double-pointed needles.

This is a very quick knit, and a classic hat that looks good on everyone. It knits up quickly in a chunky yarn.

SIZES

	Kids/Small	Women's/Medium	Large
Band circumference	16 inches/ 40 cm	17 inches/ 42.5 cm	18.25 inches/ 45.5 cm
Depth	7.75 inches/ 19.5 cm	8.75 inches/ 22 cm	9.75 inches/ 25 cm

Choose hat size based on band circumference. Band should be about 4 inches smaller than head circumference to ensure a good fit. Depth of hat is adjustable to suit a wearer with lots of hair!

MATERIALS
1(1, 1) x 100gm skein Berroco Vintage Chunky (50% acrylic, 40% wool, 10% nylon, 130yds per 100g skein). Sample uses color 6167, Dewberry
1 16 inch (40cm) 5mm (US #8) circular needle
1 16 inch (40cm) 6mm (US #10) circular needle
1 set 6mm (US #10) double-pointed needles
Stitch marker
Safety pin or removable stitch marker

GAUGE
15 sts and 20 rounds = 4 ins by 4 ins/10 cm by 10 cm in stockinette stitch using 6mm needles

METHOD
Using the smaller circular needle and the long-tail method, cast on 60 (64, 68) sts. Place a marker and join for working in the round.

Ribbing round: *K1, p1; rep from * to end of round. Remember to check if your round is twisted at this point!

Repeat ribbing round until piece measures 1 (1.25, 1.5) inches from cast-on edge.

Change to larger circular needle.
Increase round: *K2, m1; rep from * to end of round. 90 (96, 102) sts. I recommend the M1Z here.

Work even in stockinette stitch until hat measures 5 (5.75, 6) inches from cast-on edge. If the wearer has lots of hair, work 1 inch further.
Crown:
Note: The instructions are slightly different for each size. Make sure you follow the appropriate directions. When the circumference of the hat gets too small to work comfortably on the circular needle, change to the 6mm/US #10 double pointed needles

QUICK TIP

Four or Five?

Sets of double-pointed needles manufactured in (or for) the North America and the UK often come in sets of four; European and Japanese sets have five. In North America and the UK, knitters tend to distribute the stitches across three needles and use a fourth to work around; European and Japanese knitters tend to distribute the stitches across four needles and use a fifth to work around. There's no difference in the finished result — it's entirely personal preference. When starting out, most knitters find that it's a little easier to work with four rather than five.

If you've got a lot of stitches, an extra needle gives you some more space.

Many of the wooden or bamboo needles come in sets of 6 — providing a spare or two in case any get broken!

and place the safety pin or removable stitch marker in the fabric to keep track of the start of the round.

Sizes Small ONLY:

Crown round 1: *K6, s2kpo, k6; rep from * to end of round. 78 sts.
Crown rounds 2, 4, 6, 8, 10, 12: Knit.
Crown round 3: *K5, s2kpo, k5; rep from * to end of round. 66 sts.
Crown round 5: *K4, s2kpo, k4; rep from * to end of round. 54 sts.
Crown round 7: *K3, s2kpo, k3; rep from * to end of round. 42 sts.
Crown round 9: *K2, s2kpo, k2; rep from * to end of round. 30 sts.
Crown round 11: *K1, s2kpo, k1; rep from * to end of round. 18 sts.
Crown round 13: S2kpo 6 times. 6 sts.

Size Medium ONLY:

Crown round 1: *K6, s2kpo, k7; rep from * to end of round. 84 sts.
Crown rounds 2, 4, 6, 8, 10, 12, 14: Knit.
Crown round 3: *K5, s2kpo, k6; rep from * to end of round. 72 sts.
Crown round 5: *K4, s2kpo, k5; rep from * to end of round. 60 sts.
Crown round 7: *K3, s2kpo, k4; rep from * to end of round. 48 sts.
Crown round 9: *K2, s2kpo, k3; rep from * to end of round. 36 sts.
Crown round 11: *K1, s2kpo, k2; rep from * to end of round. 24 sts.
Crown round 13: *S2kpo, k1; rep from * to end of round. 12 sts.
Crown round 15: S2kpo 3 times. 6 sts.

Size Large ONLY:

Crown round 1: *K7, s2kpo, k7; rep from * to end of round. 90 sts.
Crown rounds 2, 4, 6, 8, 10, 12, 14: Knit.
Crown round 3: *K6, s2kpo, k6; rep from * to end of round. 78 sts.
Crown round 5: *K5, s2kpo, k5; rep from * to end of round. 66 sts.
Crown round 7: *K4, s2kpo, k4; rep from * to end of round. 54 sts.
Crown round 9: *K3, s2kpo, k3; rep from * to end of round. 42 sts.
Crown round 11: *K2, s2kpo, k2; rep from * to end of round. 30 sts.
Crown round 13: *K1, s2kpo, k1; rep from * to end of round. 18 sts.
Crown round 15: S2kpo 6 times. 6 sts.

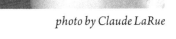
photo by Claude LaRue

Finishing
Cut yarn, leaving an 8-inch tail and pull through final sts to secure. Weave in ends. Wash.

ESSENTIAL WRIST WARMERS

These wrist warmers use a simple thumb created with a little bit of shaping but not so much that you need to really focus, making them a very quick and easy knit. With the hat, they make a nice set for yourself or for a gift.

Special skills: binding off in ribbing

SIZES:

	Teen/Women's Small	Women's Large
Palm circumference	7.25 inches	7.75 inches
Length	7 inches	8 inches

MATERIALS:
1(1, 1) x 100gm skein Berroco Vintage Chunky (50% acrylic, 40% wool, 10% nylon, 130yds per 100g skein). Sample uses color 6167, Dewberry
1 set 6mm (US #10) double-pointed needles
1 7mm or 8mm (US #11) needle for binding off
Safety pin or removable stitch marker

GAUGE
15 sts and 20 rounds = 4 ins by 4 ins/10 cm by 10 cm in stockinette stitch using 6mm needles

METHOD
Using the long-tail method, cast on 22 (24) stitches onto a single needle. Distribute across three needles as evenly as possible, and join for working in the round. Remember that you are at the start of the round when your working yarn and the yarn tail from the cast on are lined up.

Ribbing round: *K1, p1; repeat from * to end of round. Remember to check if your round is twisted at this point!

Repeat the Ribbing round 3 (4) more times.

Size Small ONLY: Next round, increase: K3, m1, k5, m1, k6, m1, k5, m1, k3. 26 sts.
Size Large ONLY: Next round, increase: K3, (m1, k6) 3 times, m1, k3. 28 sts.

Knit 10 (12) more rounds even.

Next round, create thumbhole: Bind off 3 (4) sts, knit to end.
Next round: Cast on 4 (5) sts over gap, knit to end of round. 27 (29) sts.

Work 5 (6) more rounds even.

Next round: K3, k2tog, knit to end of round. 26 (28) sts.
Work 5 (6) more rounds even.

Size Small ONLY: Next round, decrease: (K2, k2tog, k3, k2tog, k2, k2tog) twice. 20 sts.
Size Large ONLY: Next round, decrease: (K3, k2tog, k2, k2tog, k3, k2tog) twice. 22 sts.

Cuff round: *K1, p1; repeat from * to end of round.
Repeat Cuff round 8 (10) more times. Bind off using the larger needle in your right hand, in the ribbing pattern. That is, continue working the ribbing as you bind off, knitting the knit stitches, and purling the purl stitches, and lifting the stitches over as normal.

Weave in ends to finish & wash.

WARM TWO-LAYER MITTENS

I live in a cold, cold part of the world, and it's a sad truth that a basic hand-knit mitten isn't sufficiently warm for most of the winter. The challenge is that a knit fabric has little holes in, and the wind can blow through.

My simple solution is a double-layer mitten in an especially warm yarn. The inner mitten is knitted in a slightly finer yarn on larger than usual needles, making for a light and heat-trapping lining; the outer mitten is knitted in a thicker yarn on slight smaller than usual needles, making a denser fabric to stop the wind. Worn together, you have the ideal mitten.

I've used two yarns in the same family for this design, an extra-warm alpaca blend. Make sure you match gauge for the outer mitten—any standard worsted weight yarn will work. For the inner mitten, there's a fairly broad scope for substitution. Choose something in a sport or double-knitting weight range that's soft and delicious—as long as you match gauge, it doesn't matter if the fabric is a bit floppy.

If you're lucky enough to live somewhere warmer than me, then just follow the instructions for the inner mitten but work with the heavier yarn.

Special stitches used: M1R and M1L.

SIZES
Women's S, Women's M, Women's L/Men's Small, Men's Medium, Men's Large
To fit hand circumference: 7.25, 7.75, 8.25, 8.75, 9.25 inches
Hand length is fully adjustable to fit.

MATERIALS
1 (1, 2, 2, 2) skeins Berroco Ultra Alpaca Light (50% Super Fine Alpaca, 50% Peruvian Wool, 144yds/50gm). Sample uses color 4201, Winter White
1 (1, 1, 1, 2) skeins Berroco Ultra Alpaca (50% Super Fine Alpaca, 50% Peruvian Wool, 215yds/100gm). Sample uses color 6261, Ultramarine.
1 set 3.5mm (US #4) double pointed needles
1 set 4mm (US #6) double pointed needles
2 stitch markers

GAUGE
22 sts and 32 rows = 4 x 4 inches/10 x 10 cm in stockinette in the round with Ultra Alpaca and 4mm needles, for outer mitten
23 sts and 34 rows = 4 x 4 inches/10 x 10 cm in stockinette in the round with Ultra Alpaca Light and 4mm needles , for inner mitten
2 stitch markers
A 12 inch length of scrap yarn—smooth, and a contrasting color - and darning needle for thumb stitches

QUICK TIP

When a pattern tells you to rejoin the yarn, how to do it? My preferred method is as follows: knit the first stitch with the loose yarn; knit the second stitch with both ends of the yarn, and then continue with only the ball end of the yarn for the rest of the stitches. When working the double-stranded stitch, treat it as one. A nice secure join with no knots or fuss.

METHOD

OUTER MITTEN—Make 2 Alike

Cuff
Using smaller needles and heavier yarn (Ultra Alpaca), with long-tail method, cast on 38 (40, 44, 46, 50) sts. Distribute across three needles as evenly as possible, and join for working in the round. Remember that you are at the start of the round when your working yarn and the yarn tail from the cast on are lined up.

Ribbing round: *K1, p1; repeat from * to end of round. Remember to check if your round is twisted at this point!

Repeat the Ribbing round until cuff measures 2.5 (2.75, 2.75, 3, 3) inches.

Change to larger needles and work an increase round as follows:
First Size: *(K5, m1) 3 times, k4, m1; rep from * once more to end of round. 46 sts.
Second Size: (K5, m1) 8 times. 48 sts.
Third Size: (K5, m1, k6, m1) 4 times. 52 sts.
Fourth Size: *(K6, m1) 3 times, k5, m1; rep from * once more to end of round. 54 sts.
Fifth Size: *(K8, m1) twice, k9, m1; rep from * once more to end of round. 56 sts.

Thumb setup round: K2, place marker, k to end of round.
Thumb increase round: M1R, k to marker, M1L, slip marker, k to end of round. 2 sts increased.
Work 1 round even.
Repeat the last 2 rounds 5 (6, 7, 7, 8) more times. 58 (62, 68, 70, 74) sts.
Work a thumb increase round. 2 sts increased.
Work 2 rounds even.
Repeat the last 3 rounds 1 (1, 1, 1, 1) more time. 62 (66, 72, 74, 78) sts.
Next round, put thumb stitches on hold: Thread scrap yarn onto darning needle and run through first 18 (20, 22, 22, 24) sts. Knit to end of round. 44 (46, 50, 52, 54) sts.
Following round, cast on over thumb gap: Using backwards loop method (otherwise known as the M1Z), cast on 2 sts, and k to end of round. 46 (48, 52, 54, 56) sts.

Knit even in rounds until mitt from top of cuff measures 4.5 (5, 5.5, 6, 6.5) inches, or reaches to top of little finger.
Setup for decrease: K1 stitch from first needle of round onto last needle of round. Then rearrange your stitches so that there are 23 (24, 26, 27, 28) sts on the first needle, 11 (12, 13, 13, 14) on the second, and 12 (12, 13, 14, 14) on the third.

(This step ensures your thumb is centered properly at the side of the hand, and so that the decreases are positioned at the sides of the palm for a nice smooth closure.)

Decrease round: K1, ssk, k to 3 sts before end of first needle, k2tog, k1; k1, ssk, k to 3 sts before end of third needle, k2tog, k1.
Work 1 round even.
Repeat the last 2 rounds until 10 (8, 8, 10, 8) sts rem.
Cut yarn, leaving an 8-inch tail and pull through final sts to secure.

Thumb
Slip 18 (20, 22, 22, 24) sts from scrap yarn back onto two needles, divided half and half. Facing RS of mitten, starting at first thumb stitches, rejoin yarn (leaving an 8-inch tail) and knit across thumb stitches. Cast on 2 sts at end. 20 (22, 24, 24, 26) sts. Distribute them across three needles as evenly as possible and knit in rounds until thumb measures 1.25 (1.5, 1.75, 2, 2) inches from where you rejoined the yarn. (Don't worry if you lose track of the start of the round for the thumb—it really doesn't matter for this.)

Decrease round 1: (K2tog, k1) 6 (7, 8, 8, 8) times, k2tog 1 (0, 0, 0, 1) times, k 0 (1, 0, 0, 0). 13 (15, 16, 16, 17) sts.
Decrease round 2: K2tog 6 (7, 8, 8, 8) times, k 1 (1, 0, 0, 1). 7 (8, 8, 8, 9) sts.
Decrease round 3: K2tog 3 (4, 4, 4, 4) times, k 1 (0, 0, 0, 1). 4 (4, 4, 4, 5) sts.
Cut yarn, leaving an 8-inch tail and pull through final sts to secure.

Finishing
Using yarn tail, sew up little opening at base of thumb. Weave in ends. Wash.

INNER MITTEN—Make 2 Alike

Cuff
Using smaller needles and finer yarn (Ultra Alpaca Light), with long-tail method, cast on 36 (38, 42, 44, 48) sts. Distribute across three needles as evenly as possible, and join for working in the round. Remember that you are at the start of the round when your working yarn and the yarn tail from the cast on are lined up.

Ribbing round: *K1, p1; repeat from * to end of round. Remember to check if your round is twisted at this point!

Repeat the Ribbing round until cuff measures 2.5 (2.75, 2.75, 3, 3) inches.

Change to larger needles and work an increase round as follows:
First Size: *(K9, m1) 4 times. 40 sts.
Second Size: (K9, m1, k10, m1) twice. 42 sts.
Third Size: (K10, m1, k11, m1) twice. 46 sts.
Fourth Size: (K11, m1) 4 times. 48 sts.
Fifth Size: *(K12, m1) 4 times. 52 sts.

Thumb setup round: K2, place marker, k to end of round.
Thumb increase round: M1R, k to marker, M1L, slip marker, k to end of round. 2 sts increased.
Work 2 rounds even.
Repeat the last 3 rounds 5 (6, 7, 7, 7) more times. 52 (56, 62, 64, 68) sts.
Fourth and Fifth Sizes only: Work a thumb

increase round. Work 1 round even. – (–, –, 66, 70) sts.
Fifth Size only: Work a thumb increase round. Work 1 round even. – (–, –, –, 72) sts.

Next round, put thumb stitches on hold: Thread scrap yarn onto darning needle and run through first 14 (16, 18, 20, 22) sts. Knit to end of round. 38 (40, 44, 46, 50) sts.
Following round, cast on over thumb gap: Using backwards loop method (otherwise known as the M1Z), cast on 2 sts, and k to end of round. 40 (42, 46, 48, 52) sts.

Knit even in rounds until mitt measures 4.5 (5, 5.5, 6, 6.5), or reaches to top of little finger.
Setup for decrease: K1 stitch from first needle of round onto last needle of round. Then rearrange your stitches so that there are 20 (21, 23, 24, 26) sts on the first needle, 10 (10, 11, 12, 13) on the second, and 10 (11, 12, 12, 13) on the third. (This step ensures your thumb is centered properly at the side of the hand, and so that the decreases are positioned at the sides of the palm for a nice smooth closure.)

Decrease round: K1, ssk, k to 3 sts before end of first needle, k2tog, k1; k1, ssk, k to 3 sts before end of third needle, k2tog, k1.
Work 1 round even.
Repeat the last 2 rounds until 8 (10, 10, 8, 8) sts rem.
Cut yarn, leaving an 8-inch tail and pull through final sts to secure.

Thumb
Slip 14 (16, 18, 20, 22) sts from scrap yarn back onto two needles, divided half and half. Facing RS of mitten, starting at first thumb stitches, rejoin yarn (leaving an 8-inch tail) and knit across thumb stitches. Cast on 2 sts at end. 16 (18, 20, 22, 24) sts. Distribute them across three needles as evenly as possible and knit in rounds until thumb measures 1.25 (1.5, 1.75, 2, 2) inches from where you rejoined the yarn. (Don't worry if you lose track of the start of the round for the thumb—it really doesn't matter for this.)

Decrease round 1: (K2tog, k1) 5 (6, 6, 7, 8) times, k2tog 0 (0, 1, 0, 0) times, k 1 (0, 0, 1, 0). 11 (12, 13, 15, 16) sts.
Decrease round 2: K2tog 5 (6, 6, 7, 8) times, k 1 (0, 1, 1, 0). 6 (6, 7, 8, 8) sts.
Decrease round 3: K2tog 3 (3, 3, 4, 4) times, k 0 (0, 1, 0, 0). 3 (3, 4, 4, 4) sts.
Cut yarn, leaving an 8-inch tail and pull through final sts to secure.

Finishing
Using yarn tail, sew up little opening at base of thumb. Weave in ends. Wash.

WHAT'S NEXT

MAGIC LOOP

Some knitters don't like using double-pointed needles; knitters who do a lot of away-from-home knitting—on public transport, while waiting at the dentist office, in the park on a sunny day—worry about dropping or losing a needle.

Magic loop is a very clever technique to allow you to knit small circumferences on a single circular needle. You will need a circular needle with a much longer cable than usual—typically an 80cm/32 inch needle—then you will divide the stitches up half and half, pulling the cable through as .

There are videos and articles in other books on this technique. The first and best book on the subject is a little self-published booklet called *The Magic Loop* by Bev Galeskas with Sarah Hauschka. You can find it online.

Knitting Magic Loop

Chapter 8: Socks

INTRODUCTION

Socks—the most practical thing you can knit. Sock knitting is rewarding, fun, and for many knitters, a favorite project. Sock knitting can be easy and comforting, or challenging and engaging—there's a pattern to meet your every knitting mood. Sock knitting is very portable, making it an ideal travel or commuting project. I always have a sock on the needles. No matter how many other things I'm working on, I can always tuck a sock project in my purse. It's a great way to pass those idle minutes waiting at the dentist office, at the train station, at the airport, on the bus, while on hold on the telephone—anytime, any place!

There are two common ways to knit a sock—from the cuff down to the toe or from the toe up to the cuff. This chapter explains and has examples of both.

THE ANATOMY OF A SOCK

The cuff is the top of the leg of the sock. There's typically some ribbing, to stop the top from rolling down and to help keep the sock up.

The leg can be worked plain, in stockinette stitch, or in a pattern. Ribbing and cable patterns are popular, as they tighten up the fabric a bit and therefore improve the fit. A typical women's calf-length sock has a leg about 6 to 7 inches long; a man's sock has a leg about 7 to 8 inches long. (Knee socks are a different animal.)

The heel has two components: the flap, which runs down the back of the heel, and the actual heel turn, which sits under your heel. It's called a turn as it does actually change the direction of the knitting. On the leg of the sock, the rounds are running around the leg, parallel to the floor; on the foot of a sock, the rounds are running around the foot, perpendicular to the floor.

The gusset is the portion of the foot immediately beside the edges of the heel flap. Many socks will have extra fabric in this area so that they fit better. Most people have an interesting symmetry in their feet: they are roughly the same circumference around the ball of their foot as around the narrowest part of the ankle, and sock patterns are typically designed with this in mind. However, most people have a larger circumference around the arch of their foot, just beside the heel.

To accommodate that, sock patterns usually provide extra fabric for the arch, known as the gusset. (The formal definition of gusset is a triangular insert of fabric.)

SKILLS TAUGHT

Top-down and toe-up sock constructions, including band heel turn and short row heel turn.

SPECIAL STITCHES USED: Ktbl, wrap and turn.

OTHER SKILLS: Picking up stitches, Judy's Magic Cast on, Russian Lace bind off, hiding wraps, mock cable ribbing pattern.

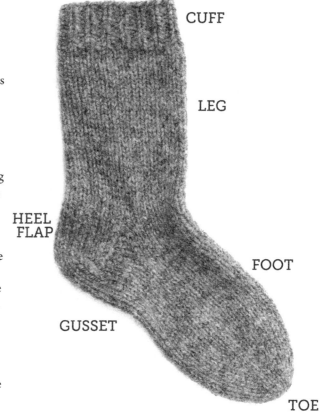

CUFF

LEG

HEEL FLAP

FOOT

GUSSET

TOE

Commercial socks typically don't have a gusset, since that construction is more complex and more difficult to create by machine. They rely on the fabric being sufficiently stretchy to be able to fit well around all parts of your foot.

The bottom of the foot is known as the sole, and the top of the foot is known as the instep. And the toe is pretty self-explanatory!

TOP-DOWN CONSTRUCTION

WHERE TO START

I like to start new sock knitters with a top-down sock first: it's easier to get started. Once you've knitted a couple of socks in each style, you can decide which you prefer based on how you enjoy the process, and how the socks fit you.

The top-down sock starts at the cuff, and the leg is worked plain in rounds until the heel flap. The flap is worked in rows on half the stitches (give or take one or two), sometimes with a pattern stitch, sometimes plain.

The heel turn is worked on the heel stitches, and the actual turn is created with decreases. My socks use a band heel, which forms a rectangular "band" under the heel. There are other types of heel turns—I like the fit of this, and find it easy to work.

Stitches are then picked up along the sides of the heel flap to reunite the round. At this point, there are more stitches than were originally cast on, to accommodate the arch of the foot. These extra stitches are decreased slowly, forming the gusset shaping. Once back to the original number of stitches, the sock is worked even in rounds until it's long enough for the toe—usually about two inches short of full foot length—and then the toe is decreased.

There are a number of opinions on the proper finish for a top-down sock. I like to finish up the toe of my socks like a hat: by decreasing down to a small number of stitches and then threading the yarn through the final stitches and pulling to close.

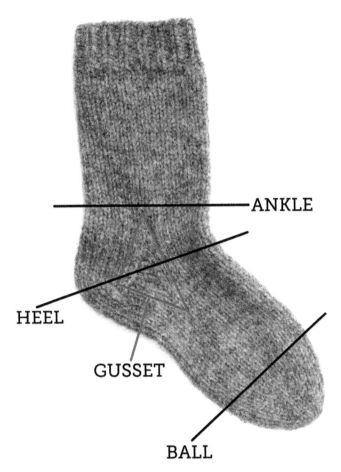

ANKLE

HEEL

GUSSET

BALL

Other knitters feel that Kitchener stitch (also known as grafting) is a better finish. Grafting is a bit more challenging, and I don't usually do it. The difference, honestly, is not major—and after all, we're talking about sock toes, which are rarely seen in public! To learn more about Kitchener stitch, consult one of the reference books listed in the bibliography.

TOE-UP CONSTRUCTION

The toe-up sock starts at the toe; some (mine included) start at the very tip of the toe, working in rounds straight away; others start with a small portion worked flat, in rows, and joined for working in the round later.

Increases are worked from the toe until you have enough stitches to go around your foot. The sock is worked even in rounds until you need to turn the heel—anywhere from about 2 to 4 inches short of the full foot length, depending on the pattern. If the sock pattern has a gusset, increases are worked on the sole portion to widen the sock to fit around the arch. The heel is then turned, working back and forth in rows. The second half of the heel turn forms a sort of flap to run up the back of the heel, but it's typically shorter than on a top-down sock. Once the heel is turned, you return to working in rounds until the leg is the length you want. Some ribbing at the top makes for a good finish.

Not all toe-up socks have a gusset; my pattern does, as I prefer the fit. If there isn't a gusset, I find that there's just not enough fabric to stretch around my heel—I either end up with a sock that fits my foot but is too tight in the heel, or a sock that fits the heel but is too loose around the foot. If you are knitting for a foot with a flatter arch, then you might find that a gusset isn't needed.

NEEDLE CHOICES

Some knitters like to knit their socks on double-pointed needles; others prefer working with two circular needles or magic loop. My training sock pattern is written specifically for double-pointed needles. My other patterns don't demand a specific needle configuration—work with whichever you prefer.

ON SOCK YARN

Not all yarn is suitable for socks. Of anything you might knit, socks are going to take the most abuse. You need to choose a yarn that will be hardwearing, one that will stand up to all the friction that comes from being pushed around in your shoes as you walk.

Most socks are knitted with a yarn made specifically for the purpose. It's known as fingering weight, and is reasonably fine, knitting up to a gauge between 28 and 32 sts per 4 inches on needles in the range of US #1 to #2 (2.25m to 2.75mm). This thickness of yarn produces socks that are likely to fit comfortably in your shoes.

Yarn made for sock knitting has two key characteristics: it's spun quite tightly, so that it wears better, and with very few exceptions, it's machine washable. Think twice about buying a sock yarn that's marked as hand wash only—are you prepared to do that?

The hardest wearing sock yarns are made from a blend of wool and nylon—sometimes called polyamide. I will choose to knit with natural fibers where I can, but nylon is an excellent addition to sock yarn. A nylon and wool blend will wear much better than a wool-only blend. I do use 100% wool sock yarns, but I'm more careful with the resulting socks—I don't put them in the dryer, and I avoid wearing them in my winter boots, or in situations where they are going to suffer a lot of friction or movement in my shoes, like a long run or a cross-country ski expedition.

Part of the fun of sock knitting is the yarn. You don't need much: unless you're knitting for very very large feet (or making knee socks), you only need 100gm. It's entirely affordable: one ball of sock yarn is much less expensive than a sweater's quantity of yarn. And the yarns themselves are quite varied and wonderful!

You can get solid-colored yarns, semi-solid yarns, yarns dyed to create very specific stripes, or even fake Fair Isle patterns. You can get yarns with strong or subtle color changes as well as stripes that change often or rarely. You can even get sock yarns made so that it's impossible to get a pair precisely the same.

You can't always tell from looking at the yarn how it's going to knit up—but then that's part of the fun with sock knitting.

I've used three very different types of color patterned yarns in the three sock patterns in the book. The first sock is made with a strongly variegated yarn with short lengths of each color, changing frequently. The second sock is made with a monochrome variegated yarn that changes color infrequently, with gentle gradations between the colors. And the third is a hand-dyed yarn with an in-between color change frequency, but more tonal changes. Each is as different as it is wonderful.
Have fun with the yarns—don't be limited by the types I've chosen.

One word of advice: a yarn with lots of color changes and vibrant colors is best used in a plain sock; make sure that socks with patterned stitches like lace and cables can be seen to best effect by using a yarn with more subtle color changes. But when working a plain sock, go color wild!

MINI PROJECT: THE TRAINING SOCK

Special stitches used: slipping stitches, ktbl.
Other skills: picking up stitches.

FINISHED MEASUREMENTS
Foot is about 4 inches long, leg is about 3 inches long to bottom of heel.

MATERIALS
scrap of worsted weight yarn (less than 25gm)
4.5mm (US #7) double-pointed needles—set of 4 or 5
Stitch holder
Safety pin

GAUGE
20 sts and 28 rounds = approximately 4 ins by 4 ins/10 cm by 10 cm in stockinette stitch using 4.5mm needles. It really doesn't matter for this project.

METHOD
Cuff
Using the long-tail method, cast 24 stitches onto a single needle. Distribute stitches evenly across 3 needles. Join for working in the round.
Ribbing round: (K1, p1) to end. Remember to check if your round is twisted at this point.

You can keep track of the start or the round by watching the tails—when the two yarn tails are lined up, you're at the start of the round.

Repeat ribbing round 5 more times.
Leg round: Knit.
Repeat leg round 5 more times.
Heel Flap
Knit 12 stitches. These will be the heel stitches.

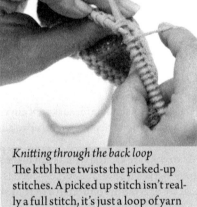

Knitting through the back loop
The ktbl here twists the picked-up stitches. A picked up stitch isn't really a full stitch, it's just a loop of yarn wrapped around your needle, and it doesn't have the structured base of a proper stitch. Knitting the stitch through the back loop "ktbl" twists the picked-up stitches to reinforce them.

Slide the remaining 12 stitches to a stitch holder—they are on hold for now, we'll come back and get them later.

Tip: In this section, you'll be slipping stitches at the starts of the rows. If you're on a RS row, slip the stitch by putting the right needle in like you're going to knit the stitch, and just sliding off the left needle. No need to wrap the yarn or pull it through. If you're on a WS row, make sure the yarn is at the front and put the needle in like you're going to purl and slip the stitch to the right needle. (Some knitters prefer to slip purlwise on both the RS and WS rows, but I find my variation makes a tidier edge.) These slipped stitches will help us with a later step.

Continuing only on the 12 heel stitches, turn so that the WS is facing and work as follows:
Row 1 [WS]: Sl 1, p11.
Row 2 [RS]: Sl 1, k11.

Repeat rows 1 & 2 twice more, and row 1 one more time

Turn Heel
Right side will be facing.

Heel row 1 [RS]: Knit 8 stitches, SKP, turn. (There will be 2 sts left at the end of the row—ignore them, we'll come back and get them later.)
Heel row 2 [WS]: Slip 1, p4, p2tog, turn. (There will be 2 sts left at the end of the row again—ignore those, too.)
Heel row 3 [RS]: Slip 1, k4, SKP, turn. (The decrease uses up one of the 2 stitches you abandoned at the end of row 1.)
Heel row 4 [WS]: Slip 1, p4, p2tog, turn. (The decrease uses up one of the 2 stitches you abandoned at the end of row 2.)
Heel row 5 [RS]: Slip 1, k4, SKP, turn. (The decrease uses up the second of the 2 stitches you abandoned at the end of row 1.)
Heel row 6 [WS]: Slip 1, p4, p2tog, turn. (The decrease uses up the second of the 2 stitches you abandoned at the end of row 2.)
At this point you will have 6 stitches, and the right side will be facing.

Shape the Gusset
Knit the 6 heel stitches.
Using the same needle, pick up and knit 6 stitches down the first side of the heel flap, using the loops created by the slipping at the start of the heel flap rows.

Using a new needle, knit across the 12 instep stitches.

Using another needle, pick up and knit 6 stitches up the second side of the heel flap, using the loops created by the slipping at the start of the heel flap rows.
Tip: I figure out where to start by counting up from the bottom.

Using that same needle, knit 3 from the heel stitches.

Decrease the Gusset
You should have 30 stitches in total: 9 stitches each on Needles 1 and 3, and 12 on Needle 2. It's common convention in sock knitting to consider the center of the heel to be the start of the round. You're in that position now. Put a safety pin in the fabric of the heel to help guide you.

Gusset setup round: K3, ktbl 6, k12, ktbl 6, k3. To work ktbl, knit the stitch through the back loop.

The ktbl here twists the picked-up stitches. A picked-up stitch isn't really a full stitch, it's just a loop of yarn wrapped around your needle, and it doesn't have the structured base of a proper stitch. Twisting the picked-up stitches reinforces them.

When picking up stitches along the edge of the heel flap, avoid the gap that occurs between the heel and the instep stitches. Although it might be very tempting to do so, picking up stitches there results in a hole.

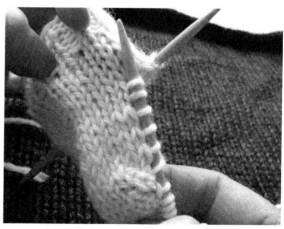

Once you've run out of slipped stitches on the edge of the heel flap, pick up and knit the additional stitches continuing along the same vertical line in the leg of the sock.

Work a decrease round:
Needle 1: Knit to last 3 stitches, k2tog, k1.
Needle 2: Knit all 12 stitches.
Needle 3: K1, ssk, knit to the end of the round.
2 stitches decreased. There should now be 8 on each of Needle 1 and 3, and 12 on Needle 2.

Work an even round.

Repeat the last 2 rounds until 6 stitches remain on each of Needle 1 and 3. 24 stitches total.

Foot
Knit 6 rounds even.

Toe Shaping
Work a decrease round:
Needle 1: Knit to last 3 stitches, k2tog, k1.
Needle 2: K1, ssk, knit to last 3 stitches, k2tog, k1.
Needle 3: K1, ssk, knit to end of needle.
4 stitches decreased. There should now be 5 on each of Needle 1 and 3, and 10 on Needle 2.

Work an even round.

Repeat the last 2 rounds until 8 stitches remain in total. Leaving an 8-inch tail, cut yarn. Finish by pulling yarn through remaining stitches.

CLASSIC TOP-DOWN SOCK

(*As pictured on facing page.*) The essential sock. Ideal for busy self-striping or variegated yarns, or for when you need an easy knit. I use this pattern all the time—everyone needs a classic in their repertoire.

I've used a wildly striped yarn for this sock—pattern stitches would just get lost with this sort of yarn. Stockinette stitch lets the colors fly. This particular yarn is hand-dyed, and has short lengths of color, hence the random striping and color "bursts."

Special stitches used: slipping stitches, ktbl.
Other skills: picking up stitches.

If you're familiar with the magic loop method, you can use it here. If you aren't, I've provided a reference on where to learn more in the "What's Next" section on page 64.

SIZES
Women's S (shoe size 5–7), Women's M (shoe size 7½–9), Women's L (shoe size 9½+), Men's S (shoe size 6–9), Men's L (shoe size 9½+)

Note on choosing a size: foot length is entirely customizable. For a wide foot, go up a size and then just knit the foot longer; for a very narrow foot, go down a size and knit the foot shorter.

MATERIALS
Approx. 100gm/400m fingering weight sock yarn. Samples use Blue Moon Fiber Arts' Socks That Rock Lightweight (100% superwash merino, 360 yds per 126gm skein) in "Knitters Without Borders" color. If you're using this yarn, you will need a second skein for the larger sizes (Women's L, and all men's sizes), as the yardage isn't generous.
1 set 2.5 mm (US #1.5) needles—double-pointed needles, or a long circular as you prefer
1 stitch holder (optional)
Stitch markers (for working on circular needles)

GAUGE
30 sts and 44 rounds = 4 ins by 4 ins/10 cm by 10 cm in stockinette stitch in the round using 2.5 mm needles

METHOD
Cuff and Leg
Using the long-tail method, cast 56 (60, 64, 64, 68) stitches onto a single needle. If you're working on double-pointed needles, distribute sts evenly across 3 needles; if you're working on a long circular with the magic loop method, divide the stitches so that half are on one needle tip, half on the other. Join for working in the round, being careful not to twist.

Ribbing round: (K1, p1) to end of round. Tip: if you prefer, work K2, p2 ribbing for the cuff.

Remember to check if your round is twisted before you proceed. You can keep track of the start or the round by watching the tails—when the two yarn tails are lined up, you're at the start of the round.

Repeat this round until sock measures 5cm/2 inches from cast on.

Next round: Knit all sts.
Repeat this round until sock measures 6.5 (7, 8, 8, 8) inches from cast-on edge.

Turn Heel
This portion is knitted flat.

Heel row 1 [RS]: Knit first 28 (30, 32, 32, 34) stitches onto one needle and turn so that WS is facing. Put remaining 28 (30, 32, 32, 34) stitches onto a holder. From here, you'll continue only on the first half of the round.
Heel row 2 [WS]: Slip 1, p27 (29, 31, 31, 33), turn.
Heel row 3 [RS]: Slip 1, k27 (29, 31, 31, 33), turn.
Heel row 4 [WS]: Slip 1, p27 (29, 31, 31, 33), turn.
Repeat the last 2 rows 9 (10, 11, 12, 12) more times. The right side is facing for next row.

Heel turn row 1 [RS]: K19 (20, 21, 21, 23), SKP, turn.
Heel turn row 2 [WS]: Slip 1, purl 10 (10, 10, 10, 12), p2tog, turn.
Heel turn row 3 [RS]: Slip 1, knit 10 (10, 10, 10, 12), SKP, turn.
Heel turn row 4 [WS]: Slip 1, purl 10 (10, 10, 10, 12), p2tog, turn.

Repeat the last 2 rows until all stitches have been worked. Ensure right side is facing for next row. 12 (12, 12, 12, 14) stitches remain on the needle.

Re-establish Round and Create Gusset
Knit all stitches. Using that same needle, pick up and knit 15 (16, 17, 17, 18) stitches along selvedge edge at side of heel, using slipped stitches as a guide. With a new needle, work across the 28 (30, 32, 32, 34) stitches of instep—those stitches that you'd set aside on the stitch holder. Using a new needle, pick up and knit 15 (16, 17, 17, 18) stitches along selvedge edge at other side of heel, using slipped stitches as a guide. Work 6 (6, 6, 6, 7) stitches from the first needle, to the center of the heel.

The beginning of the round is now at the center of the heel. If you're working on magic loop, place a marker in this position.

There should be 21 (22, 23, 23, 25) sts between the start of the round and the start of the instep, 28 (30, 32, 32, 34) stitches on the instep, and 21 (22, 23, 23, 25) between the end of the instep and the end of the round. 70 (74, 78, 78, 84) sts total. Rearrange the stitches if you need to. If you're working on double-pointed needles, those first 21 (22, 23, 23, 25) sts should be on your first needle, the instep sts on your second needle, and the other 21 (22, 23, 23, 25) sts on the third needle. If you're working magic loop, the instep sts should be on one needle, and the other stitches on a second needle, with a marker for the start of the round at the mid-point.

Decrease Gusset
Gusset setup round: K6 (6, 6, 6, 7), ktbl 15 (16, 17, 17, 18), k 28 (30, 32, 32, 34) instep sts, ktbl 15 (16, 17, 17, 18), k to end of round.
Gusset decrease round: Knit to three stitches before start of instep, k2tog, k1. Knit across instep sts. K1, ssk, k to end of round. 2 sts decreased.
Following round: Knit.
Repeat these last two rounds until 56 (60, 64, 64, 68) stitches rem total on your needles—14 (15, 16, 16, 17) each side between the start of round and the instep stitches and 28 (30, 32, 32, 34) instep stitches.
Foot
Work until foot measures 6.5 (7, 7.5, 7.5, 8.5) inches, or 2.5 inches less than foot length. (Note that the finished sock should be a little shorter than the foot. This makes for a better fit.)

Shape Toe

Toe decrease round: Knit to three stitches before start of instep, k2tog, k2, ssk; k to 3 sts before end of instep, k2tog, k2, ssk, k to end of round. 4 sts decreased. Note: the instep sts will be together on their own needle, so you can keep track of the decrease positions that way.

Work 3 rounds even.
Work a decrease round followed by 2 even rounds, twice. [6 rounds total]
Work a decrease round followed by 1 even round, three times. [6 rounds total]
Work decrease rounds until 8 stitches remain.

To finish, cut yarn, draw through the final stitches and tighten. Weave in ends.

CLASSIC TOE-UP SOCK

(*As pictured on page 77*). The other basic—worked the other way around.

I've used a different sort of self-striping yarn, with much longer sections of color between changes. When it came time to work the heel, I pulled the yarn from the center of the ball—this allows the color changes to run uninterrupted along the foot and up into the leg.

Special stitches used: Judy's Magic Cast on (see pages 74–75); Russian Lace bind off.
Other skills: wrap and turn; hiding wraps.

If you're familiar with the magic loop method, you can use it here. If you aren't, I've provided a reference on where to learn more in the "What's Next" section (page 64).

SIZES:
Women's S (shoe size 5-7), Women's M (shoe size 7½-9), Women's L (shoe size 9½+), Men's S (shoe size 6-9), Men's L (shoe size 9½+)
Note on choosing a size: foot length is entirely customizable. For a wide foot, go up a size and then just knit the foot longer; for a very narrow foot, go down a size and knit the foot shorter.

MATERIALS:
Approx. 100gm/400m fingering weight sock yarn. Samples use Zauberball Crazy (75% superwash wool, 25% nylon, 459yds per 100gm ball) in color 2099.
1 set 2.5 mm (US #1.5) needles—double-pointed needles or a long circular as you prefer
2 safety pins or removable stitch markers
2 other stitch markers
1 stitch holder (optional but helpful)

GAUGE
32 sts and 44 rounds = 4 ins by 4 ins/10 cm by 10 cm in stockinette stitch using 2.5 mm needles

METHOD
Using Judy's Magic Cast On, cast on 20 (20, 24, 24, 24) sts – 10 (10, 12, 12, 12) on each of two needles.

If you're working on double-pointed needles, start as follows:
Round 1: K5 (5, 6, 6, 6) with one needle, k5 (5, 6, 6, 6) with a second needle, and k10 (10, 12, 12, 12) with a third. The first stitch may be loose—twist the tail around the working yarn when you work it. (*Pattern continues on p. 76.*)

QUICK TIP

Wrap & Turn:

On the right side, slip the next stitch purlwise onto the right-hand needle; move the working yarn to the front, slip the stitch from the right needle back to the left needle and turn so that the wrong side is facing. Move the yarn to the front so that you're in position to purl.

On the wrong side, slip the next stitch purlwise onto the right-hand needle; move the working yarn to the back, slip the stitch from the right needle back to the left needle and turn so that the right side is facing. Move the yarn to the back so that you're in position to knit.

QUICK TIP

Working Wrapped Stitches Together with Their Wraps:

On the right side: put the tip of the right needle under the front of the wrap, and knit it together with the stitch it wrapped.

To work the ssk with the wrap: with the tip of the right needle up onto the left needle, then slip both the wrap and the stitch together to the right needle — these together count as the first slipped stitch of the ssk. Then slip the next stitch and complete the ssk as normal.

On the wrong side: put the tip of the right needle under the back of the wrap (that is, on the right side of the knitting), and lift the wrap up onto the left needle. Purl the wrap together with the stitch it wrapped.

To work the p2tog with the wrap: put the tip of the right needle under the back of the wrap (that is, on the right side of the knitting), and lift the wrap up onto the left needle. Purl the wrap together with the stitch it wrapped and the following stitch.

JUDY'S MAGIC CAST-ON

This is the key cast-on for toe-up socks. It provides a stable base so the first few rounds are easy to knit, and a nice flat seam so that the toes don't rub and irritate your feet.

1. Set up the yarn as if for working a long-tail cast-on, with a slip knot on one needle. Hold two needles together in your right hand, as per the long-tail cast on; the needle that has the slip knot should be on the right.

2. Swing the needles over to the right, and over top of the right strand. Wrap the right strand over the left needle so that the yarn runs down between the two needles.

3. Swing the needles over to the left and over top of the left strand. Wrap the left strand over the right needle so that the yarn runs down between the two needles.

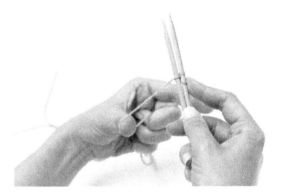

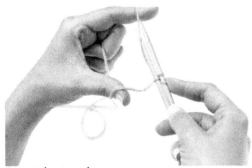

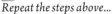

Repeat the steps above...

Repeat these two steps until you've got the right number of stitches on each needle.

If you look at the underside of the needles, you'll see "purl bumps" between the needles. This helps you keep track of which is the right and which is the wrong side.

For more details, take a look at the original article on Knitty: http://www.knitty.com/ISSUEspring06/FEATmagiccaston.html

If you're working with magic loop or 2 circulars, start as follows:
Round 1: K10 (10, 12, 12, 12) sts with one needle, and k10 (10, 12, 12, 12) with a second. The first stitch may be loose—twist the tail around the working yarn when you work it.

No matter which needle configuration you're using, this first round will be fiddly. Don't worry if it's difficult to work.

Place a safety pin or marker in the toe to indicate the start of the round, and a second to indicate the center of the round.

For all methods, continue as follows:

Work an increase round: K1, m1, knit to 1 st before center of round, m1, k2, m1, knit to 1 st before end of round, m1, k1.
Knit 1 round even.

The round should be more stable at this point, and easier to knit.

Repeat the above two rounds until you have 56 (60, 64, 64, 68) sts total on your needles.

Foot round: Knit.
Repeat this round until sock measures 6.5 (6.75, 7.5, 7.75, 8) inches from tip of toe.

Shape Gusset
Setup round: Knit to center of round; on needle containing second half of round m1, pm, knit to end of round, pm, m1.
Note: You will have half the stitches between the two markers. I recommend the M1Z here.
Round 2: Knit all stitches.
Round 3: Knit to first marker; m1, sl m, knit to second marker, sl m, m1, knit to end.
Round 4: Knit all stitches.

Repeat rounds 3 & 4 4 (4, 5, 5, 6) more times. 68 (72, 78, 78, 84) stitches total.

The Short Row Gusset Heel
This is worked back and forth in rows on half the sock stitches—specifically, on the stitches in the second half of the round, between the markers. Note: You may wish to slip all the instep stitches to a holder at this point.

At this point, if you want to, start working with the other end of the ball.
Setup round [RS]: Knit to first marker, slip marker, knit to 1 st before second marker, wrap and turn.
Row 2 [WS—working only on the stitches between the markers]: Purl to 1 st before marker, wrap and turn.

Working only on the heel stitches, continue:
Row 3 [RS]: Knit to st before last wrapped st, w&t.
Row 4 [WS]: Purl to st before last wrapped st, w&t.

Repeat Rows 3 & 4 until 10 (10, 12, 12, 12) sts remain unwrapped in the middle, ending with a WS row.

Work the heel flap, reducing the gusset stitches as you go:
Row 1 [RS]: Knit to first wrapped stitch, *knit the wrapped st together with its wrap; rep until 1 wrapped st remains, and work an ssk on this final stitch together with its wrap AND the first of the gusset stitches. Turn.

Row 2 [WS]: Slip 1, purl to first wrapped st, *purl the wrapped st together with its wrap; rep from * until 1 wrapped st remains, and purl this final st together with its wrap AND the first of the gusset stitches. Turn.

Row 3 [RS]: Slip 1, k to 1 st before gusset stitches, ssk, turn.
Row 4 [WS]: Slip 1, p to 1 st before gusset stitches, p2tog, turn.
Repeat the last 2 rows 3 (3, 4, 4, 5) more times until all but one of gusset stitches on each side have been decreased. 58 (62, 66, 66, 70) stitches rem. RS will be facing.

If you changed yarn at the start of the heel, change back now.
Leg and Cuff
From here, you will restart working in rounds, in stockinette stitch. The two final gusset decreases are worked in the round—I find it makes

the top of the heel neater, and the join smoother.

First leg round, final decreases: K to 1 st before the first of the two final gusset sts, ssk. K to 1 st before the last gusset st, k2tog.

Work even until leg measures 5.5 (6, 7, 7, 7) inches from the top of the heel.

Ribbing round: *K1, p1; repeat from * to end of round. Repeat ribbing round for 2.5 cm/1 inch.

Bind off very very loosely, using the Russian Lace bind off as follows: K2, *slip these two stitches purlwise back onto the left needle, k2tog, k1; repeat from * until a single stitch remains. Break yarn and pull the end through to secure. This bind off is nice and stretchy.

TOP-DOWN BASIC RIBBED SOCK

(*As pictured on page* 79). I love the look of a sock with a ribbed leg, and ribbing does improve the stretchiness and therefore the fit, but I find large sections of knit 1/purl 1 ribbing fairly tedious. Knit 3/purl 1 is much more interesting!

For this, I've used a tonally dyed hand-dyed yarn with medium lengths of color so that the overall effect is more shaded rather than striped. If you're familiar with the magic loop method, you can use it here. If you aren't, I've provided a reference on where to learn more in the "What's Next" section (page 64).

Special stitches used: slipping stitches, ktbl.
Other skills: picking up stitches.

SIZES
Women's S (shoe size 5-7), Women's M (shoe size 7½-9), Women's L (shoe size 9½+),
Men's S (shoe size 6-9), Men's L (shoe size 9½+)

Note on choosing a size: foot length is entirely customizable. For a wide foot, go up a size and then just knit the foot longer; for a very narrow foot, go down a size and knit the foot shorter.

MATERIALS
100 gm/400m sock yarn—sample uses Sweet Georgia BFL Sock (80% superwash blue-faced Leicester wool, 20% nylon, 375yds/115gm skein) in color Autumn Flame.
1 set 2.5 mm (US #1.5) needles—double-pointed needles or a long circular as you prefer
1 stitch holder (optional)
Stitch marker (for working on circular needles)

GAUGE
40 sts and 44 rows, unstretched = 4 inches/10cm in (k3, p1) rib with 2.5mm needles.

METHOD
Cuff
Using the long-tail method, cast 56 (60, 64, 64, 68) sts onto a single needle. If you're working on double-pointed needles, distribute sts evenly across 3 needles; if you're working on a long circular with the magic loop method, divide the stitches so that half are on one needle tip, half on the other. Join for working in the round, being careful not to twist.

Ribbing Round: (K3, p1) to end of round.
Remember to check if your round is twisted before you proceed. You can keep track of the start or the round by watching the tails—when the two yarn tails are lined up, you're at the start of the round.
Repeat Ribbing Round until sock measures 6.5 (7, 8, 8, 8) inches.

Turn Heel
This portion is worked flat.
Heel flap row 1 [RS]: Work 27 (27, 31, 31, 35) sts in ribbing pattern as established. Put remaining 29 (33, 33, 33, 33) sts onto a holder if desired. Turn so that WS is facing.
Heel flap row 2 [WS]: Slip 1, work 26 (26, 30, 30, 34) sts in ribbing pattern, turn.
Heel flap row 3 [RS]: Slip 1, work 26 (26, 30, 30, 34) sts in ribbing pattern, turn.
Heel flap row 4 [WS]: Slip 1, work 26 (26, 30, 30, 34) sts in ribbing pattern, turn.

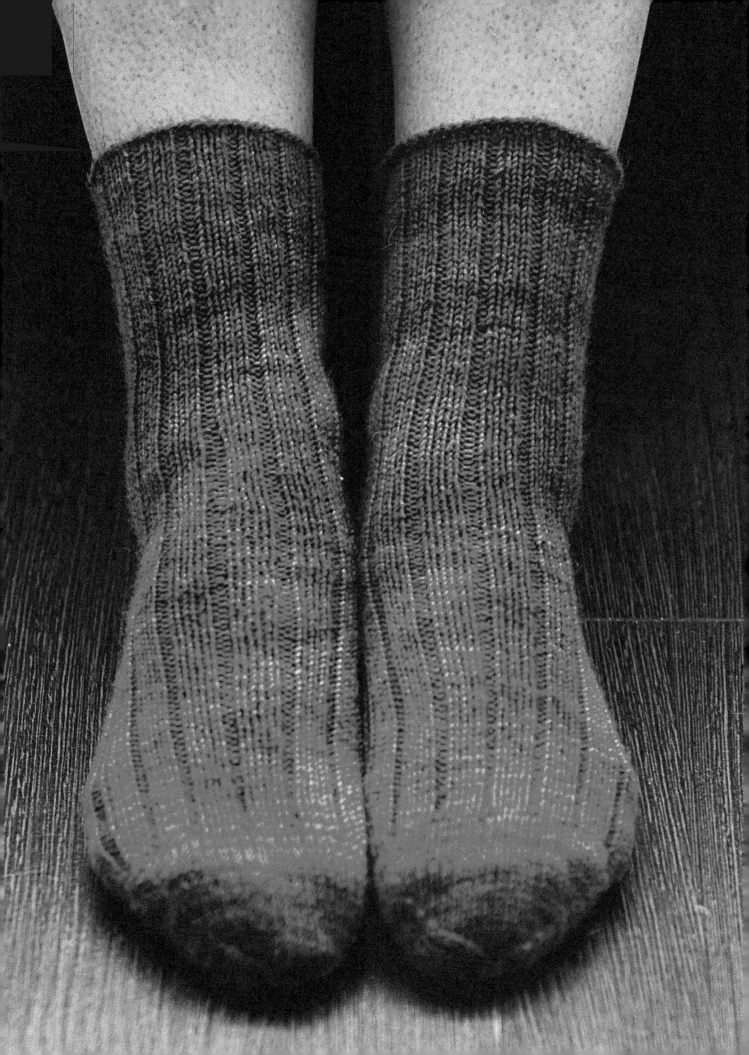

Repeat the last 2 rows 9 (10, 11, 12, 12) more times. The right side is facing for next row.

Heel turn row 1 [RS]: Knit 18 (18, 21, 21, 23) sts, ssk, turn.
Heel turn row 2 [WS]: Slip 1, purl 9 (9, 11, 11, 11) sts, p2tog, turn.
Heel turn row 3 [RS]: Slip 1, knit 9 (9, 11, 11, 11) sts, ssk, turn.
Heel turn row 4 [WS]: Slip 1, purl 9 (9, 11, 11, 11) sts, p2tog, turn.

Repeat the last 2 rows until all sts have been worked. 11 (11, 13, 13, 13) sts remain, and RS is facing.

Re-establish Round and Create Gusset
Knit all heel sts. Using that same needle, pick up and knit 15 (16, 17, 17, 18) sts along selvedge edge at side of heel, using slipped sts as a guide. With a new needle, work in rib pattern across the 29 (33, 33, 33, 33) sts of instep—those sts that you'd set aside on the stitch holder. (The instep sts should start and end with a purl stitch.) Using another new needle, pick up and knit 15 (16, 17, 17, 18) sts along selvedge edge at other side of heel, using slipped sts as a guide. Work 6 (6, 7, 7, 7) sts from the first needle, to the center of the heel.

The beginning of the round is now at the center of the heel. If you're working on magic loop, place a marker in this position.

There should be 20 (21, 23, 23, 24) sts between the start of the round and the start of the instep, 29 (33, 33, 33, 33) stitches on the instep, and 21 (22, 24, 24, 25) between the end of the instep and the end of the round. 70 (76, 80, 80, 82) sts total. Rearrange the stitches if you need to. If you're working on dpns, those first 20 (21, 23, 23, 24) sts should be on your first needle, the instep sts on your second needle, and the other 21 (22, 24, 24, 25) sts on the third. If you're working on two circulars or magic loop, the instep sts should be on one needle, and the other stitches on a second needle, with a marker for the start of the round at the mid-point.

From here on in, the 29 (33, 33, 33, 33) instep sts will be worked in the rib pattern, and the gusset and sole will be worked in stockinette stitch—that is, knitting every stitch every round.

Decrease Gusset
Gusset setup round: K5 (5, 6, 6, 6), ktbl 15 (16, 17, 17, 18), work across the instep sts in pattern as established, ktbl 15 (16, 17, 17, 18), k to end of round.
Gusset decrease round: K to 2 sts before instep, k2tog, work across instep sts in pattern, ssk, k to end of round.
Work an even round, keeping ribbing pattern on instep.
Repeat these last two rounds until Needle 1 has 13 (13, 15, 15, 17) sts and Needle 3 has 14 (14, 16, 16, 18) sts. 56 (60, 64, 64, 68) sts total on your needles.

Foot
Work until foot measures 6.5 (7, 7.5, 7.5, 8.5) inches, or 2.5 inches less than foot length. (Note that the finished sock should be a little shorter than the foot. This makes for a better fit.)

Shape Toe
From here on in, you'll work entirely in stockinette stitch. Rearrange the sts so that you've got 28 (30, 32, 32, 34) on the sole and 28 (30, 32, 32, 34) on the instep. If you're working magic loop, you will have the same number on each needle; if you're working on double-pointed needles, divide the stitches of the sole evenly across two needles.

Toe decrease round: Knit to three stitches before start of instep, k2tog, k2, ssk; k to 3 sts before end of instep, k2tog, k2, ssk, k to end of round.
Work 3 rounds even.
Work a decrease round followed by 2 even rounds, twice. [6 rounds total]
Work a decrease round followed by 1 even round, three times. [6 rounds total]
Work decrease rounds until 8 stitches remain.
To finish, cut yarn, draw through the final stitches and tighten. Weave in ends.

DESIGNING YOUR OWN

Using the basic sock patterns I've provided, you can start making your own designs. Change the ribbing. Work a pattern stitch all the way around the leg. Add a cable running down the front of sock, in the center of the instep.

Adding a pattern stitch to the leg is the easiest way to customize your socks: choose something that divides up evenly into the number of stitches you have on your sock. All of the sock patterns I provide are worked on multiples of four stitches, so you can choose stitch patterns that are multiples of two or four.

Mock Cable Rib

For example, I'm very fond of the mock cable ribbing for socks:

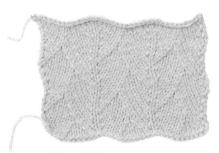

Mock Cable Ribbing Pattern (Over a multiple of 4 sts, worked in the round)
Rounds 1 and 2: *K2, p2; rep from * to end.
Round 3: *Skip first stitch (leaving it in place on the needle) and k into second stitch, then k into first and slip both off the needle at the same time, p2; repeat from * to end of round.
Round 4: As Round 1.

It's as easy to work as a regular ribbing pattern, and creates a really sophisticated look. And it's easy to cheat! If you would normally use 56 stitches for your sock, but you want to use a pattern stitch that's a multiple of 12 stitches, cast on 60 sts for the leg, and then in the final round of the leg before you start the heel flap, work a decrease round to get you down to 56 stitches.

Dragon Skin

I love this texture pattern, known as "Dragon Skin", as it creates a really great scalloped effect in the fabric.

Round 1: *K1, m1, ssk, k4, k2tog, k3, m1; repeat from * to end of round.
Round 2 and all even rounds: Knit.
Round 3: *K1, m1, k1, ssk, k2, k2tog, k4, m1; repeat from * to end of round.
Round 5: *K1, m1, k2, ssk, k2tog, k5, m1; repeat from * to end of round.
Round 7: *K1, m1, k3, ssk, k4, k2tog, m1; repeat from * to end of round.
Round 9: *K1, m1, k4, ssk, k2, k2tog, k1, m1; repeat from * to end of round.
Round 11: *K1, m1, k5, ssk, k2tog, k2, m1; repeat from * to end of round.

When applying a pattern stitch, there's a few things to keep in mind: cables tend to tighten up the knitting; lace loosens it up. If adding cable patterns, you might need more stitches; if using lace patterns, you will likely want fewer stitches for the leg. Of course, if you work the leg with a different number of stitches than you would normally, make sure you increase or decrease as necessary to get the right number before you start the heel.

WHAT'S NEXT

Take a look at sock patterns that incorporate pattern stitches—lace and cables are common, and make for fun knitting and beautiful results.

GREAT SOCK KNITTING BOOKS

Nancy Bush has written a few terrific sock knitting books, although be careful about her sizing. Many of her sock patterns only come in one size. Look for *Knitting Vintage Socks, Folk Socks,* and *Knitting on the Road.*

If toe-up sock knitting tickles your fancy, check out the work of Wendy D. Johnson. Her most recent book is *Socks from the Toe Up: Essential Techniques and Patterns from Wendy Knits.*

Clara Parkes' *The Knitter's Book of Socks* is an excellent addition to the literature, providing not only beautiful patterns but also lots of detail about yarn choices and practical tips for knitting socks that are comfortable to wear and that last a long time.

Cat Bordhi is doing incredibly innovative work re-engineering sock knitting with different constructions and shapes. Some of it's pretty challenging, but it's all definitely worth exploring. Start with *New Pathways for Sock Knitters, Book One,* and then take at look at *Personal Footprints for Insouciant Sock Knitters.*

Chapter 9: Cables

INTRODUCTION

When many people think of hand-knitted garments, they think first and foremost of Aran sweaters—those lovely cabled sweaters associated with Ireland. Many knitters love how cables look, but are intimidated by them: they look like they're difficult to work, and the patterns can seem very complex. Cables are actually surprisingly easy to work, and once you know how to read them, the patterns are entirely straightforward. In this chapter we'll deal with both challenges.

Cables are, at their essence, just ribs. The classic rope cable consists of a knit rib with purls on either side, and every so often the knit rib is twisted.

All that's happening with the twist is that stitches are crossed over each other: you're swapping the positions of stitches.

In the example in the photograph, there are 8 stitches in the knit rib. The first four stitches of the knit rib are moved behind and to the left, and stitches 5, 6, 7, and 8 are moved in front and to the right.

WORKING A CABLE

It looks complicated, but this swapping of stitches is achieved in the simplest way imaginable: you slip the first 4 stitches to a cable needle—just like a little stitch holder. Easy!

Slipping sts to cable needle

Holding the cable needle to the back

Working the next 4 sts.

All of the wonderful different patterns come from different permutations and combinations: different numbers of stitches and twists in different directions; sometimes it's all knits, sometimes it's knits and purls. That's it!

After performing the three steps above, you will slip the stitches from the cable needle back to the left hand needle and continue to knit the rest of the row. The first and simplest variation is the direction of the turn: by slipping stitches to the cable needle and holding that needle to the back, the left-most stitches become the about-to-be-worked stitches and thus travel to the right, over the top of the stitches on the cable needle. This results in a cable that seems to twist from left to right. If you hold the slipped stitches to the front, the resulting cable seems to twist from right to left.

Some knitters don't bother returning the held stitches to the left-hand needle, they work the stitches directly from the cable needle. It's entirely personal preference. I prefer to take that extra step, I find that it helps me keep things even and tidy, and it's easier for me to work the stitches.

The key is to ensure that you're moving the stitches on and off in the same order—you don't want to twist them around.

Cables are turned every few rows: typically, as often as there are stitches. For example, an 8-stitch cable is turned every 8 rows: the other 7 rows of the pattern it's just plain old ribbing.

>*Row 1 [RS]: K8.*
>*Row 2 [WS]: P8.*
>*Row 3 [RS]: Slip next 4 stitches to cable needle and hold in back, k4, then k4 from cable needle.*
>*Row 4 [WS]: P8.*
>*Row 5 [RS]: K8.*
>*Row 6 [WS]: P8.*
>*Row 7 [RS]: K8.*
>*Row 8 [WS]: P8.*

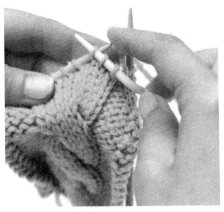

You can cross the cable to the left by holding the cable needle in the front:

A four stitch cable is turned every 4 rows, e.g.:

>*Row 1 [RS]: K4.*
>*Row 2 [WS]: P4.*
>*Row 3 [RS]: Slip next 2 stitches to cable needle and hold in front, k2, then k2 from cable needle.*
>*Row 4 [WS]: P4.*

Of course, every rule gets broken, and some patterns turn the cables more or less often than you'd expect for visual effect. A cable turned less often makes for a softer, more relaxed look in your fabric. A cable turned more often makes for a tighter, twistier look.

Cables do cause your knitted fabric to contract; you're pulling the stitches over each other, which tightens up the ribs. More cables turned more often snug up the fabric a lot; a few cables turned infrequently don't significantly change the fabric.

EQUIPMENT

There are a few different styles of cable needle. My personal favorite is the shepherd's hook style, for two reasons. Because the two ends are different lengths, it's easy to keep track of which way you should be slipping the stitches: they go on and off the same end. In addition, this style of needle is easily stored when you're not using it— simply hook it on the neckline of your t-shirt or the edge of your knitting bag!

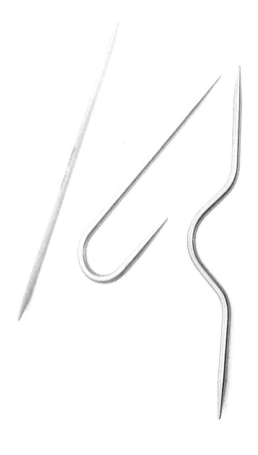

Some knitters don't use anything special: a short double-pointed needle serves well as a cable needle, too. I've even seen a golf tee used, in a moment of desperation. Contrary to popular wisdom, I like to use a cable needle that's larger than the needles I'm working with: the stitches are less likely to slip off while being held. Some knitters don't use a cable needle at all; see the "What's Next" section for information on where to learn more about that technique.

READING THE PATTERNS

The bigger challenge with cables is reading the patterns: they add a whole new set of terms and abbreviations—but once you understand the basic rules, you're good!

First things first: cn stands for cable needle.

The instructions tell you everything you need to do: how many stitches to work with, and where to hold the cable needle, and what to do with the stitches. In the pattern rows themselves, an abbreviation is often used, but there is always—ALWAYS—an explanation of the abbreviation provided somewhere in the pattern.

For example, in the coffee cup cozy pattern (page 87) , you see the abbreviation C8R. Below the 8 rows of the pattern C8R is explained as follows: C8R: *Slip next 4 sts to cn and hold in back; k4, then k4 from cn.* Everything you need to know!

There is a method to the madness in the abbreviations: C stand for cable, 8 is the number of stitches you'll be working with, and R is the direction in which the cable turns—right, in this case. So you might see C6L, for example, indicating that you're working with 6 stitches, the completed cable turns to the left, and it is worked as follows: *C6R: Slip next 3 sts to cn and hold in front; k3, then k3 from cn.*

Sometimes, you'll see C8B or C6F, instead. F and B are used to indicate where you hold the cable needle—front or back.

Although these are the most commonly used standards for cable instructions, there can be minor variations. If you're not sure what's required—indeed, even if think you are sure—just check the table of abbreviations for the pattern. It might be on the same page, or it might be in a master list somewhere in the back of the book, but it's always there (and if you can't find one, it's a sign that perhaps the pattern is poorly written and may contain even more serious errors).

Designers use these abbreviations—C8R, C4L—because it *does* make the patterns easier to read: if we wrote out the instructions every time, you'd end up with very very long pattern rows.

For example, instead of ...
Row 1 [RS]: K2, p2, slip next 4 sts to cn and hold in back; k4, then k4 from cn, p2, slip next 4 sts to cn and hold in front; k4, then k4 from cn, p2, slip next 4 sts to cn and hold in back; k4, then k4 from cn, p2, k2.

... you have the much tidier and easier to read:
Row 1 [RS]: K2, p2, C8R, p2, C8L, p2, C8R, p2, k2.

CHARTS

As discussed previously, charts are simply visual representations of pattern instructions. Some knitters prefer charts, some knitters prefer the written instructions. Use whichever you like best!

Symbols used for cables are the full width of the cable—8 stitches wide for an 8-stitch cable, for example. Although there are several different styles, all contain the same basic elements: an indication of how many stitches are worked and the direction in which the cable turns.

I like charts because they provide a visual representation of how the cable is to look. It's hard to guess what is going to happen when you read the rows of a pattern that are written out, but the chart gives you a good sense of the end result.

A 4-stitch rope cable might be charted as follows (see right):

You can easily see here that the cable on the right side twists to the left, and the cable on the left twists to the right, with purl stitches in between. And as with any chart, always look for the legend.

(For more details on reading charts, see page 30.)

VARIATIONS: NUMBERS OF STITCHES

You can cross as many stitches as you like over as many stitches as you want to. I've mentioned crossing 3 over 3 (C6L, C6R) and crossing 4 over 4 (C8L, C8R), but there are no limits. 2 over 2 is pretty common (C4L, C4R), and I've crossed cables as narrow as 1 stitch over 1 stitch and as wide as 24 stitches (12-over-12, C24R, C24L). The bigger the cable, of course, the more your knitting pulls in, but anything is possible.

And although it's common convention for cables to be symmetrical, there's absolutely no need: you can cross 2 stitches over 1, making for a less extreme cross. It would be worked as follows: Slip next 2 sts to cn and hold in front, k1, then k2 from cn, abbreviated typically as C3L.

purl

C4L

C4R

knit

VARIATIONS: CROSSING KNITS OVER PURLS

In all the above examples, all the stitches in the cables are knit stitches, but this isn't always the case. Sometimes, you work combinations of knits and purl stitches as follows: *slip next 2 sts to cn and hold in back, k2, then p2 from cn.*

The effect is a rib of knit stitches travelling over a purl background. The classic Aran diamond is created this way: a knit rib moves slowly to the left and then back to the right.

A "T" is often used in the abbreviation for these stitches—standing for twist—to indicate that it is be a combination of knits and purls. The stitch above, for example, might be abbreviated as T4R or T4B.

VARIATIONS: COMBINATIONS

You also see cables in combinations—a simple left-leaning 4-stitch rope cable can become something entirely different when it's worked immediately beside a right-leaning 4-stitch rope cable.

The classic horseshoe cable is just two rope cables, next to each other, turned more frequently. And the "hugs and kisses" cable is just a variation of that: varying the direction in which the cables are turned. (See the swatches on page 87.) Those beautiful Aran sweaters are just a number of different cabled elements worked across the sweater.

WORKING CABLED PATTERNS

Cables are surprisingly easy to work, and I find them enormously satisfying.

The first few rows of a cable pattern require the most attention, as you're counting off the stitches. As with working ribbing, once you are established, you can see what needs to happen where—e.g. where you need to purl—and you'll find yourself making fast progress.

Paper and pencil are key for these patterns, to help you keep track. A classic Aran sweater might have four or five different elements on the front and the back, all being worked at the same time. The more cable elements, the more complex the knitting will be; the more you will need to pay attention.

Sometimes, you're working different elements with different numbers of rows in the repeats. They're not impossible—but they do require focus. If this is the case, I keep track of the different cables separately.

It's pretty easy to gauge the degree of difficulty of a cabled project: fewer cables, the easier it's going to be. And if there are multiple cables, it's easier if it's the same cable repeated over and over (as in the hat pattern, page 90) than if it's different cables. If a pattern has different cables, it's easier if they are similar (as in the scarf pattern, page 89), than if they are wildly different (as in the Aran sweater pictured at left).

No matter how many cables there are in a project, the knitting is rewarding and enjoyable, and the resulting look is sophisticated and attractive. Give it a go!

HORSESHOE CABLE

Over 8 sts and 8 rows.
Row 1 [RS]: K8
Rows 2, 4, 6, 8 [WS]: P8.
Row 3: C4R, C4L.
Rows 5, 7: K8.

HUGS & KISSES CABLE

Over 8 sts and 16 rows.
Row 1 [RS]: K8
Rows 2, 4, 6, 8, 10, 12, 14, 16 [WS]: P8.
Row 3: C4R, C4L.
Row 5: K8.
Row 7: C4L, C4R.
Row 9: K8.
Row 11: C4L, C4R.
Row 13: K8.
Row 15: C4R, C4L.

MINI PROJECT: COFFEE CUP COZY

Special stitches used: C8R.
Other skills: Invisible horizontal seam

Choose a color that matches how you take your coffee so spills don't show.

FINISHED MEASUREMENTS
3.25 inches/8 cm wide, 9 inches/23 cm around unstretched; will stretch easily to fit the largest take-out coffee cup.

MATERIALS
1 50gm ball Sirdar Eco Wool DK (100% undyed virgin wool, 100m/50gm ball; color 201—grey)
4 straight 4mm (US #6) needles—wood, bamboo or plastic needles are easiest
Cable needle
Yarn needle

GAUGE
22 stitches and 28 rows across 4 inches/10cm in stockinette stitch on 4mm needles.

METHOD
Cast on 20 sts.
Row 1 [RS]: K4, p2, k8, p2, k4.
Rows 2, 4, 6, 8 [WS]: K6, p8, k6.
Row 3 [RS]: K4, p2, k8, p2, k4.
Row 5 [RS]: K4, p2, C8R, p2, k4.
Row 7 [RS]: K4, p2, k8, p2, k4.

C8R: Slip next 4 sts to cable needle and hold in back; k4, then k4 from cable needle.
Repeat the last 8 rows until piece measures 9 inches long, ending after a Row 1.
Bind off, leaving a 12 inch tail which you will use for seaming.

FINISHING
Wash the piece.
With RS facing, seam using the invisible horizontal seaming method as given below, using the tail left over from the cast-off.

HOW TO WORK AN INVISIBLE HORIZONTAL SEAM

If you look closely at your knitting, you'll see that at the bottom of each knit stitch—each v—you'll see a point. You'll use these for seaming.

Fold the coffee cozy in half along the short side, with right sides facing you, and line up the cast-on and bind-off edges. The cast-off tail should be on your right if you're right-handed; on your left if you're left-handed. Thread your darning needle with your cast-off tail.

And so forth. When seaming purl stitches, the v is still there, it's just hiding a little bit. Stretch the fabric out to see the vs.

Pull snug as you work. When you get to the end, weave in your ends.

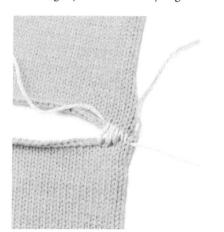

CHUNKY CABLED SCARF

(*As pictured on facing page.*) Special stitches used: C4R, C4L.

FINISHED MEASUREMENTS
One size, approx 9 inches wide and 60 inches long.

MATERIALS
1 skein Cascade Eco+ (100% wool, 478yds/250gm skein). Sample uses color 94516
4.5mm (US #7) needles—straight or short circular, as you prefer
Cable needle

GAUGE
Approximately 21 sts and 22 rows = 4 ins by 4 ins/10 cm by 10 cm in Cable Rib pattern, unstretched. Gauge isn't critical, as long as you like the fabric that results.

METHOD
Cast on 50 sts.
Row 1 [WS]: *P2, k2, p6, k2; rep from * to last 2 sts, p2.
Row 2 [RS]: *K2, p2, C4R, k2, p2; rep from * to last 2 sts, k2.
Row 3 [WS]: Repeat row 1.
Row 4 [RS]: *K2, p2, k2, C4L, p2; rep from * to last 2 sts, k2.
Work from written or chart instructions as you prefer.
C4R: Slip 2 sts to cn and hold in back, k2; then k2 from cn.
C4L: Slip 2 sts to cn and hold in front, k2; then k2 from cn.

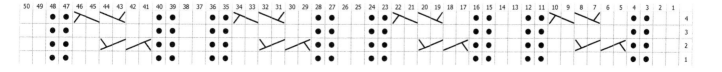

Repeat the last 4 rows until you've just about run out of yarn, or scarf is about 60 inches long, ending with a WS row. Bind off in ribbing pattern.

CABLED HAT

(*As pictured on page 88*). The same cables are used in both the hat and the scarf; in the hat, the cables are worked in the round and therefore, you need to pay a little bit more attention to count the rounds between the turns.

Special stitches used: C4R, C4L.
Other skills: working cables in the round, working decreases in cables.

MATERIALS
1 skein Cascade Eco+ (100% wool, 478yds/250gm skein). Sample uses color 9451
4.5mm (US #7) 16-inch circular needle and dpns
stitch markers—1 for start of round; others of a different style or color for dividing up repeats if you wish.

GAUGE
Approximately 20 sts and 28 rounds = 4 ins by 4 ins/10 cm by 10 cm in cable pattern, stretched
Approximately 40 sts and 28 rounds = 4 ins by 4 ins/10 cm by 10 cm in cable pattern, unstretched

Cable pattern, over 6 sts
Rounds 1, 3: K6
Round 2: C4R, k2. (Slip 2 sts to cn and hold in back, k2; then k2 from cn.)
Round 4: K2, C4L. (Slip 2 sts to cn and hold in front, k2; then k2 from cn.)

METHOD:
Using circular needle and the long-tail cast on, cast on 96 (108, 120) sts, join for working in the round, placing a marker for start of round, being careful not to twist.

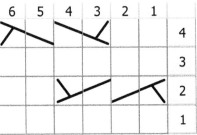

Cable pattern

Body round: *K2, p2, work cable pattern over 6 sts, p2; rep from * to end of round. Use stitch markers to divide up repeats if it helps you keep track.

Work in pattern as established, repeating 4 rounds of cable pattern, until hat measures 6.5(7, 7.5) inches from cast on edge, ending after an even-numbered round.
Note: during decrease, when hat gets too small to work comfortably on circular needle, change to dpns.

Decrease round 1: *K2tog, p2tog, continue cable pattern over next 6 sts, p2tog; rep from * to end of round. 72 (81, 90) sts.
Decrease round 2: *K1, p1, continue cable pattern over next 6 sts, p1; rep from * until 9 sts rem, k1, p1, continue cable pattern over next 6 sts, and STOP. This will be the new start of round. Move your marker.
Decrease round 3: *P2tog, p1, continue cable pattern over next 6 sts; rep from * to end of round. 64 (72, 80) sts.
Decrease round 4: *P2, continue cable pattern over next 6 sts; rep from * to end of round.
Decrease round 5: *P2tog, continue cable pattern over next 6 sts; rep from * to end of round. 56 (63, 70) sts.
Decrease round 6: *P1, continue cable pattern over next 6 sts; rep from * to end of round.
Decrease round 7: *P1, k2tog 3 times; rep from * to end of round. 32 (36, 40) sts.
Decrease round 8: *P1, s2kpo; rep from * to end of round. 16 (18, 20) sts.
Decrease round 9: P2tog around. 8 (9, 10) sts.

FINISHING
Cut yarn and draw through rem sts. Pull tight and weave in ends. Wash it.

CLASSIC CABLED SOCK

(*As pictured on page 92*). A deceptively simple cable is used to create a classic Aran-sweater inspired sock. I chose a yarn in the perfect warm winter white.

Special stitches used: C4R, T3R, T3L
Other skills: Reading cable charts; working a cable both in the round and flat.

SIZES AND FINISHED MEASUREMENTS
Women's size S fits up to shoe size 6½; size M fits up to shoe size 8½; size L fits shoe size 9+. Note that the cables pull in fairly aggressively, so that the sock will look very small unworn.

MATERIALS
2 (3, 3) balls Patons Kroy (75% wool, 25% nylon, 152m per 50gm ball). Sample uses color 55008 Muslin.
1 set 2.5 mm (US #1.5) needles—double-pointed needles or a long circular as you prefer
Cable needle
stitch markers - 2 if working on double-pointed needles, 3 if working with circular needle(s)

GAUGE
32 sts and 44 rows = 4 ins by 4 ins/10 cm by 10 cm in stockinette stitch

PATTERN NOTES
This pattern is sized in an unusual way. The basic stitch pattern is a 14-stitch repeat, and so the small features 4 repeats of the pattern and the large features 5; to provide a size in between, I've created a modified version of the cable pattern with two additional purl stitches in the repeat. The difference is barely visible in the finished socks.

METHOD
Using the long-tail cast on, cast on 56 (64, 70) sts. Distribute across your needles as you prefer and join for working in the round, being careful not to twist. It's a good idea to keep a multiple of 14 (16, 14) sts on each needle to help you keep track of the patterning.

Leg setup round: Work setup row of appropriate Cable pattern 4 (4, 5) times around.
Leg round 1: Work row 1 of appropriate Cable pattern 4 (4, 5) times around.
Leg round 2: Work row 2 of appropriate Cable pattern 4 (4, 5) times around.

Continue in pattern, repeating rows 1-20 of appropriate Cable pattern as established until 3 full repeats of the 20 rows are complete, and work another 5 (3, 3) rounds.

Heel flap setup row 1 [RS]: Work 28 (32, 35) sts in pattern as per cable pattern row 6 (4, 4). Turn so that WS is facing.

Heel flap row 2 [WS]: Sl 1, 27 (31, 33) sts in pattern as per cable pattern row 7 (5, 5), turn. Note that these 28 (32, 34) sts will be used for the heel flap—the rem 28 (32, 36) will be used for the instep. Slip them to a holder if you wish.
Heel flap row 3 [RS]: Sl 1, 27 (31, 33) sts in pattern, turn.
Heel flap row 4 [WS]: Sl 1, 27 (31, 33) sts in pattern, turn.

Continue in pattern as established until cable pattern row 7 (7, 9) is complete. 22 (24, 26) rows total in heel flap.

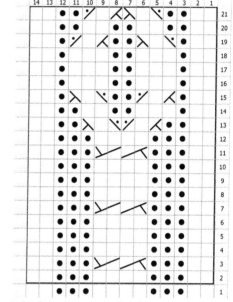

Cable for sock sizes small and large

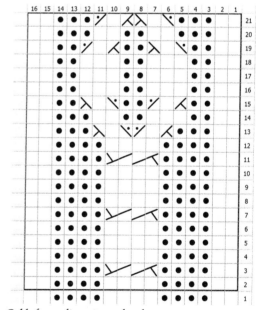

Cable for medium size sock only

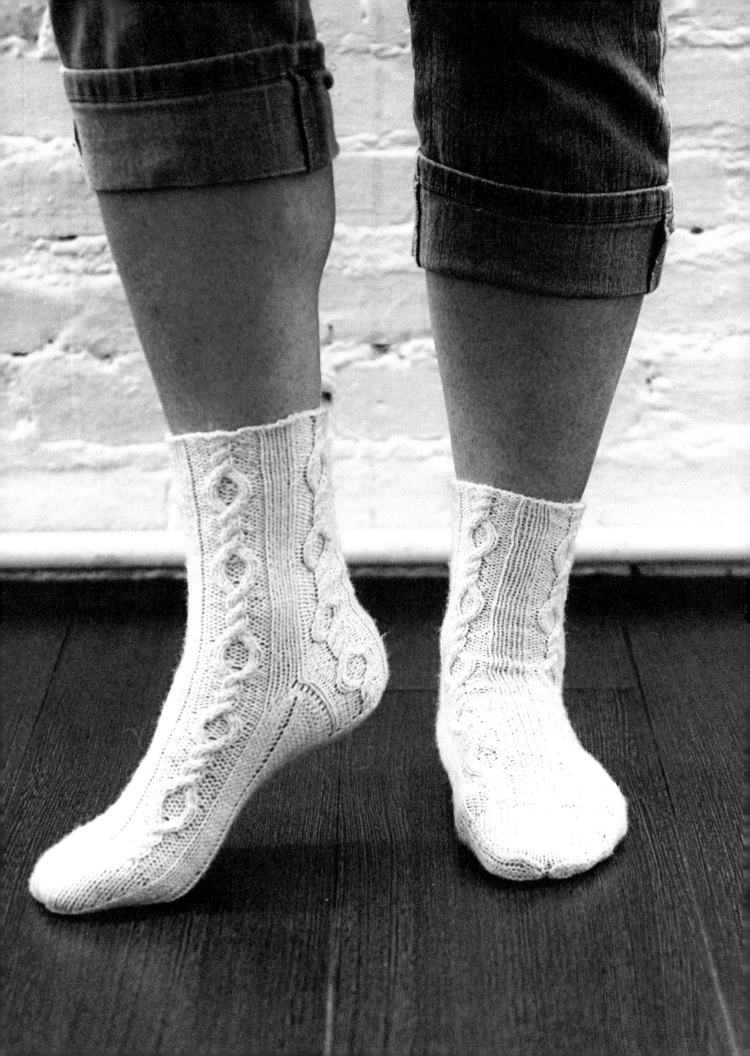

Heel turn:
Heel turn row 1 [RS]: K19 (21, 23), SKP, turn.
Heel turn row 2 [WS]: Slip 1, purl 10 (10, 12), p2tog, turn.
Heel turn row 3 [RS]: Slip 1, knit 10 (10, 12), SKP, turn.
Heel turn row 4 [WS]: Slip 1, purl 10 (10, 12), p2tog, turn.

Repeat rows 3 & 4 until all heel sts have been worked and 12 (12, 14) sts rem.

Gusset:
RS will be facing. Knit across 12 (12, 14) sts of heel.
With the same needle, pick up and knit 15 (16, 17) sts along the first side of the heel flap, using the slipped sts as a guide. Work across 28 (32, 36) held sts in pattern, starting at chart row 6 (4, 4). With a new needle, pick up and knit 15 (16, 17) sts along the second side of the heel flap, using the slipped sts as a guide. With the same needle, k 6 (6, 7) sts of the heel. This is the new start of round. Place a marker if you're working on circular needles. 70 (76, 84) sts—28 (32, 36) on instep, 42 (44, 48) on sole.

Gusset round 1: K6 (6, 7), ktbl 12 (13, 16), place marker for start of instep pattern, p1, k2 (2, 0); work across instep sts in pattern, k2 (2, 0), p1, place marker for end of instep pattern, ktbl 12 (13, 16), k 6 (6, 7). 34 (38, 38) sts between instep markers.
Gusset round 2: K to 2 sts before first instep marker, k2tog; work across 34 (38, 38) sts of instep in pattern; ssk, k to end of round.
Gusset round 3: K to first instep marker; work across 34 (38, 38) sts of instep in pattern; k to end of round.

Repeat the last 2 rounds 6 (5, 6) more times. 56 (64, 70) sts total—34 (38, 38) between the instep markers, and 22 (26, 32) sts on sole.

Foot
Work even in pattern until foot is roughly 2.25 (6cm) inches shorter than full foot length, ending with an odd-numbered cable pattern row. It looks best if you can finish after either Row 12 or Row 2 of the pattern, as that completes a motif, but it's not essential. On the final round, remove the instep markers.

Toe:
Toe setup and first decrease: K11 (13, 14), k2tog, k1, place marker for start of instep; k1, ssk, k 22 (26, 29), k2tog, k1, place marker for end of instep, k1, ssk, k 11 (13, 15) to end of round.
Knit three rounds even.
Toe decrease round: K to 3 sts before first marker, k2tog, k1, slip marker, k1, ssk, k to 3 sts before second marker, k2tog, k1, slip marker, k1, ssk, k to end of round.
Knit 2 rounds even.
Repeat the last 3 rounds.
Work a decrease round followed by 1 even round, three times. (6 rounds total).
Work only decrease rounds until 8 sts rem.

Finishing: Cut yarn and draw through rem sts. Pull tight and weave in ends. Hand wash.

WHAT'S NEXT

More complex combinations! Take a look through some stitch libraries to see what sorts of amazing patterns you can build from these basic building blocks.

- The Barbara Walker Stitch Treasuries are fabulous; and volume 2 in the Vogue Stitchionary Series is entirely focused on cables.
- For cabled garments, check out Fiona Ellis's *Inspired Cable Knits*.
- For working without a cable needle, see http://www.knitty.com/ISSUEwinter07/FEATwin07TT.html

Chapter 10: Lace

INTRODUCTION

Lace knitting is considered to be the most beautiful—and challenging—work you can do with your needles. Beautiful, absolutely. Difficult? Doesn't have to be. Lace is a very broad category—some lace knitting is indeed expert-level work, but much of it is actually very accessible. The patterns in this chapter are all designed specifically to be easy and fun to work.

THE STRUCTURE OF LACE

Lace is, very simply, deliberate holes in your knitting. The yarnover increase, as discussed in the Shaping chapter (Chapter 6), creates a hole—and adds a stitch. Lace is just lots of strategically placed yarnovers, for decorative effect.

To keep the number of stitches the same, you work a decrease every time you work a yarnover. That's it! For example, a classic and very effective lace pattern requires you to simply repeat *k2tog, yo* across a row. The huge variety of stitch patterns comes from how the decreases and the yarnovers are combined.

FISHNET LACE

Fishnet and Trellis lace are the fundamentals; the essence of lace in its simplest form, and the basis on which all lace is built.

Fishnet Lace—Right Leaning
Worked on an even number of stitches, e.g. 20.

> *Row 1 [RS]: K1, *k2tog, yo; repeat from * to last stitch, k1.*
> *Row 2 [WS]: Purl.*
> *Row 3: *K2tog, yo; repeat from * to last 2 stitches, k2.*
> *Row 4: Purl.*

Repeat the above 4 rows.

You can see that this pattern biases strongly to the right—the cast-on edge becomes slanted. This is happening because of the position of the yarnover relative to the decrease: the yarnover is after the decrease, and therefore pushes everything over to the right.

Compare this with the next swatch:

Fishnet Lace—Left Leaning
Worked on an even number of stitches, e.g. 20.

> *Row 1 [RS]: K1, *yo, ssk; repeat from * to last stitch, k1.*
> *Row 2 [WS]: Purl.*
> *Row 3: K2, *yo, ssk; repeat from * to end.*
> *Row 4: Purl.*
> *Repeat the above 4 rows.*

This biases to the left because the yarnover is ahead of the decrease, pushing the rest of the row over to the left.

In the first swatch I used k2tog, a right-leaning decrease, to create those strong, crisp, right-leaning lines. In the second I used ssk, which leans to left, to create the crisp left-leaning lines.

If you want to eliminate the bias, alternate left-leaning rows and right-leaning pattern rows, as in the Trellis Lace:

SKILLS TAUGHT

How lace is structured.
Working a lace pattern.
Use of lifelines.
Tip-up and top-down triangular shawl shaping.
Reading lace charts and blocking lace

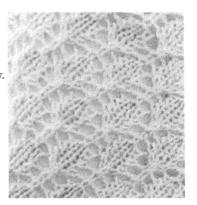

Right-leaning fishnet

Left-leaning fishnet

TRELLIS LACE

Worked on an odd number of stitches, e.g. 21.

> Row 1 [WS]: Purl.
> Row 2 [RS]: K1, *yo, k2tog; repeat from * to end of row.
> Row 3: Purl.
> Row 4: *Ssk, yo; repeat from * to last stitch, k1.

Other than the lack of bias, this lace pattern has another key difference from the previous two: you're using a left-leaning decrease on a right-leaning row, and a right-leaning decrease on a left-leaning row. This creates the waving central lines in the stitch pattern: If I'd used a left-leaning decrease on a left leaning row, and a right leaning decrease on a right-leaning row, you'd get much harder lines. Try it and see on the modified pattern below!

MODIFIED TRELLIS LACE

Worked on an odd number of stitches, e.g. 21.

> Row 1 [WS]: Purl.
> Row 2 [RS]: K1, *yo, ssk; repeat from * to end of row.
> Row 3: Purl.
> Row 4: *K2tog, yo; repeat from * to last stitch, k1.

Trellis lace

THE OTHER SIDE

All of the patterns so far have had a "rest" row—every other row is purled. This creates a lace that has a clear right and wrong side, with the plain areas in stockinette. It also provides an excellent opportunity for knitters to catch their breath, on the wrong side rows.

You can, of course, knit the wrong sides rather than purling. This gives a garter stitch background to the pattern. Although the two sides aren't precisely the same, the lace that results is reversible, and lies flat like standard garter stitch. More challenging lace pattern stitches have no rest row at all: both sides are patterned. The classic Shetland "Faggoting" stitch is worked in this way.

BASIC "FAGGOTING" STITCH

Worked on an even number of stitches, e.g. 20.

> Row 1: K1, *yo, ssk; repeat from * to last st, k1.
> Repeat Row 1.

Some older books distinguish between these two types of lace—with a plain WS row, it's called Lace Knitting, and with a pattern WS row, it's called Knitted Lace. These "knitted lace" patterns are more challenging to work, but create really wonderful results. In particular, the classic Shetland stitch pattern in the swatch above creates a look that's quite unlike knitting, and is more fascinating for it.

OTHER COMBINATIONS

Lace faggoting

All the myriad stitch patterns and designs in lace simply come from these basic rules—a yarnover increase is used to create a decorative hole, and a decrease to compensate. Directional decreases create lines of emphasis and directional waves. In all the swatches above, the decrease is right next to its yarnover companion, but that's not mandatory—there may be plain stitches between them, or they may be organized differently. In the Crest of the Wave motif used in the rectangular scarf pattern on page 100, there are four decrease and four increases in the pattern repeat—the yarnovers are grouped in the middle, and the decreases are at the start and end of the repeat. And in some more complex patterns, the decreases take place on a different row entirely! You'll also see other decreases used: the Modest Lace Shawl pattern on page 102 uses k3tog, and s2kpo is common. The stitch combination (yo, s2kpo, yo) is used a lot in Shetland lace and it's a classic building block for pattern stitches as you'll see in the Cat's Paw pattern used in the Lace Bookmark below.

You often see a left leaning decrease immediately before a right-leaning decrease, with yarnovers on either side. If repeated in the same place on multiple rows, this stitch combination has a very interesting effect: it causes a scallop in the rows, seen in the swatch at right. The decreases work together to pull the fabric up towards the center—the first decreases pulls the fabric towards the left, and the second decrease pulls the fabric towards the right. These two biases work together to create the scalloped edge. These scallops cause the rows to wave, and do wonderful things with a self-striping yarn.

The stitch pattern for this swatch is very simple, worked of a multiple of 7 sts plus 1.

> *Row 1 [RS]: K1, *yo, k1, ssk, k2tog, k1, yo, k1; rep from * to end of row.*
> *Row 2 [WS]: Purl.*

You can see the same effect in the Crest of the Wave scarf below, although it's created slightly differently. There are two k2togs at the right side of the lace motif, and two ssk decreases at the left side. This placement of decreases causes the right sides to pull up towards the right, and the left sides to pull up towards the left. There isn't a scallop in the Cat's Paw Lace bookmark because the decreases are worked in different positions in each row of the pattern.

Scallopy lace pattern

WORKING A LACE PATTERN

Lace isn't necessarily appropriate for knitting while watching TV or in the car, but it's very rewarding work for when you have the time to focus and good light to work under. Lace knitting is my favorite type of travel (bus, train, air) knitting, as it's very engaging over long stretches of time, and since it's typically worked with finer yarn, a project doesn't take up a lot of room in your bag. Whether at home or on the road, always keep paper and pencil at hand, to keep track of rows and stitches.

Crest of the Wave edging

Lace patterns are often charted. See the section on reading charts on page 30 for more help with this. The charts are helpful whether they are your preferred pattern style or not, as they give you a visual guide as you work. Of course, consulting the photograph is helpful for this, too. Even more so than other types of knitting, you need to look at your lace—often, and in great detail. The beauty of lace depends on the stitches lining up—on the decreases and yarnovers appearing at the right place in the row. Look carefully at each row to see if your pattern is aligned, and to see if what's on your needles matches the intended result.

Whether you're working from a chart or written instructions, make a photocopy and keep the instructions in a sheet protector; use sticky notes or highlighter tape to help you read the rows. Check off the rows as you go, and if you're putting your knitting down, make a note of which row you've just completed. And as you're looking at your work, count your stitches. Counting is absolutely the most important thing you can do when working lace. Because you're working increases and decreases, your stitch count is constantly changing. You need to make sure you have the same number of stitches at the end of the row that you had at the beginning—or that the pattern indicates.

When I'm working the first few rows of a pattern, I will count after every pattern row. When working a multi-row pattern, I'll count at least at the end of every complete repeat. Use markers liberally; divide up all the repeats of a pattern, even if it's only a small repeat, or it seems very simple. The markers help you keep track of where you are in the row, of course, and they are of inestimable value in helping you count your stitches.

Lace knitting is more detailed—and therefore slower—work than plain knitting. It's not necessarily the thing to pick up if you've got a deadline for a gift. Remember that as with cables, the first few rows are going to be slower as you get the pattern established, but you will pick up speed as you get to know the pattern stitch.

KNITTERLY ADVICE

Don't be afraid of trying any kind of new technique. When I was a new knitter, someone told me that cables were hard. So I carefully avoided cables for seven years after that. When I finally did try one, and discovered that it's just knitting stitches out of order, I could have screamed — seven lost years during which I could have made Aran sweaters with ease for everyone I knew... don't listen to discouraging words. Try anything you fancy the look of.

— Julia Grunau, Patternfish

The best piece of advice about lace knitting was offered by a good friend of mine. It's common sense, but we've all been known to ignore common sense from time to time: *Don't knit lace when you're tired.*

MISTAKES AND THE LIFELINE

The most daunting thing about lace knitting is that even the simplest mistake can send you off track. Lace patterns require a specific number of stitches, and losing or gaining a stitch can make a mess of your stitch patterns. You should expect at some point that you'll have to undo some of your rows. Even the most experienced knitters do, and it's not something to be ashamed of. Rather than having to go back right to the beginning every time, lace knitters make use of the lifeline.

Feeding a lifeline

After you've finished a section—a pattern repeat, for example, or a set of 10 rows—and you've determined that your stitch count is correct, feed a lifeline: take a length of a smooth, fine yarn or thread in a contrasting color, and thread it through the stitches on your needle. It's best to do it after a plain (wrong-side) row, making sure to write down which row you're on. Then just keep working!

Unwaxed dental floss or fishing line works brilliantly as a lifeline, too.

Lifeline off needle

The lifeline forms a bookmark and natural break—and brake. If something goes wrong, you can remove your knitting from the needles and undo. The lifeline stops the work from unravelling any further, and allows you to put it back on the needles intact, and start again.

Just follow the path of the lifeline when you're putting your needle back into the row.

I usually have more than one lifeline on the go: don't remove one until you know that the rows you've worked between the current row and the last lifeline are actually correct! You can remove the lifelines as you work, or leave them all in place until the project is complete. A knitter I know makes a small celebration of triumphantly removing all her lifelines from her lace after the final stitch is bind off.

Putting stitches back on needle from lifeline

All the patterns below have pointers on how to avoid—and fix—mistakes as you are working.

GAUGE, YARN CHOICES, AND NEEDLES

The great thing about lace is that gauge doesn't really matter. Being off gauge by a stitch or two isn't going to make or break a scarf; ending up with a piece slightly smaller or slightly larger than anticipated isn't really a problem.

We still swatch for gauge for lace patterns, but instead of worrying about precisely matching stitch and row counts, we do it to make sure that we like the fabric that results. Lace is typically worked with larger needles that you normally would for a given yarn, to create a drapier and looser fabric, and to allow the yarnovers to really open up and the patterning to show off. For example, traditional laceweight yarns are finer than sock yarn, and yet needles as large as 3.5mm or 4mm (US4 or 6) are often used.

There is broad scope for yarn substitution with lace patterns—without altering the pattern, a thicker yarn makes for a bigger piece; a finer yarn makes for a smaller piece. Easy! Just make sure you buy the same amount (the same distance) so you can complete the project.

Remembering that lace is typically worked with larger needles, it's tough to find a yarn substitution by looking only at the gauge given in the pattern. I tend to look at the yarn itself, and use that as a guide. If I want something to be about

YARN WEIGHT	TYPICAL NEEDLE SIZE FOR NON-LACE APPLICATIONS	NEEDLE SIZE FOR LACE
Lace weight	not typically used for anything other than lace	3-4mm
Fingering	2.25-2.75mm	3-4mm
Double knitting	3-4mm	4-5mm
Worsted	4-5mm	5-6mm

the same size, I look for a yarn that's about the same size; if I want something bigger, I look for a heavier yarn, and increase my needle size accordingly. See the table for suggested needle sizes used in lace knitting with particular yarn weights.

The yarn itself can make a huge difference in the finished project, but also in the knitting experience. Lace needs to be worked with an animal fiber (or blend containing animal fibers) so it will block out and hold the stretch.

A smoother yarn is easier to work with—and will show off the work to better effect. Although beautiful, fuzzy mohair blends are not ideal for your first lace project. Not only is it hard to see your stitches—and too easy to lose a stitch—but they are almost impossible to undo.

Many lace patterns call for yarns that are "singles"—that only have a single ply. These yarns can be more challenging to work with, as they tend to fuzz up and felt, and can be stickier and therefore harder to undo.

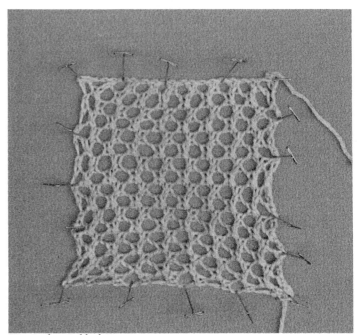

My favorite yarn for lace work is fingering weight sock yarn, or yarns categorized as "baby wools". They are fine enough to produce a lovely light piece, but not so fine that you'll damage your eyesight trying to see your stitches; they are typically machine washable wool, so that they are more easily blocked, and will hold the blocking well, and they are smooth and have multiple plies, which makes them easy to handle on your needles, and easy to undo.

The needle type can make a difference, too, with your lace knitting experience. A pointier needle is better, to help you "dig" into stitches for all the decreases. I highly recommend that you choose wood, bamboo or plastic needles for your first lace experiences. These needles are less slippery, and therefore your stitches are less likely to go sliding off as you work. I find I knit a little slower on needles with some natural friction to them, but this helps me with my lace. Even though you will find "turbo" needles on the shelves, slow and steady is definitely the watchword for lace knitting.

Pinning lace to block it

Many lace patterns, especially triangular shawls, call for circular needles—not because they are worked in the round, but so that you can handle the growing number of stitches. If your stitches are on a long circular needles, you can stretch the piece out so you can take a good look as you work—to admire, and to check for mistakes.

FINISHING LACE

Lace looks pretty terrible when it comes off your needles: it's creased and crumpled. The yarnovers collapse, and the decreases don't lie flat.

All knitting looks better if you wash it before you declare it finished, but lace really needs a finishing wash. In particular, lace needs to be blocked: washed and then stretched to shape to even out the fabric and open up at the yarnovers.

(All of the swatches photographed above have been blocked; if you've worked any of them, you'll find that your knitting likely doesn't look quite as smooth.)

The same lace pattern, blocked and unblocked

A little bit of special equipment is required for blocking lace: a laundry rack and pegs, or some pins and a surface to pin to: rubber mats (those jigsaw-puzzle shaped kids' playmats) or Styrofoam or even just a stretch of carpet that's away from the reaches of any small people or animals. Look at the washing instructions for the yarn: yarn that's machine washable can be thrown in the machine for a quick wash; yarn that's marked as hand-wash only should be soaked in lukewarm water for 15 minutes. A little bit of wool wash or appropriate soap is a good idea—especially if you tend to snack when you knit—but not mandatory.

Roll the piece in a towel to pull out most of the moisture, and then pin it out, stretched, and leave to dry. You do need to stretch fairly aggressively; the yarn shouldn't feel like it's going to break, but make sure the piece is completely flat and wrinkle-free.

This is why we typically use animal fibers (or blends with animal fibers in them) for knitting lace: wool holds its shape and stretch. Once blocked, a wool shawl will stay smooth, stretched and beautiful for a long time. It will need to be re-pinned if you wash the piece again, but most lace doesn't require frequent washing.

ANTICIPATING THE CHALLENGE LEVEL OF A LACE PATTERN

It's easy to fall in love with a lace pattern; the key to success is understanding the level of difficulty of a given pattern.

Look at how many charts there are: a pattern with a single chart is going to be easier than a pattern with three or four. And of course, the size of the chart makes a difference: a 7-stitch repeat worked over 10 rows is much easier than a 28 stitch repeat worked over 36 rows.

Look carefully at the pattern stitch—is there a plain WS row, or are both sides patterned? A plain WS row (whether knitted or purled) makes for easier knitting than a design with a patterned WS row.

Another key factor is the weight and quantity of yarn used: a design that uses 300m of a worsted weight will likely be an easier knit than a design that uses 1500m of a cobweb weight yarn. And consider, too, the type of yarn: you can make a very simple lace pattern enormously challenging with poor yarn and needle choice (I have a very sad story about a garter stitch scarf I tried to knit with a laceweight mohair on metal needles); equally, you can make a challenging lace pattern a fun learning experience by making sure that your yarn and needle choices are ones that you know will be easy to work with.

Choosing a pattern slightly beyond your comfort level is a terrific way to challenge yourself and learn new skills. Just make sure that you're well equipped with lifelines and a good light to work under—and you're not in a rush to finish it.

MINI PROJECT: LACE BOOKMARK

Special Stitches used: Yo, ssk, k2tog, s2kpo
Other skills: use of lifeline, reading lace patterns

A quick and easy lace project. Be careful about the decrease in row 7—remember that there are two with very similar names, use the correct one.

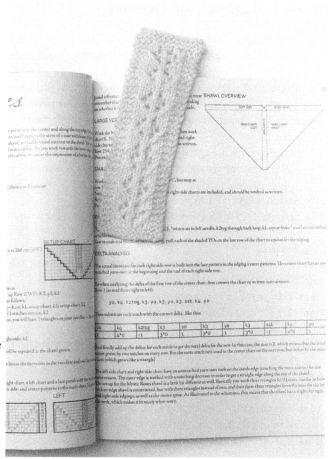

The stitch pattern is the classic and beautiful Cat's Paw. It uses pairs of directional decreases to keep the rows balanced—unbiased.

Count your stitches after every patterned row. If you make a mistake, it's easy to undo and restart.

FINISHED MEASUREMENTS
Approximately 2¼ inches/6 cm wide and 6¾ inches/17cm long.

MATERIALS
Scraps of leftover sock yarn—I used a few grams of Patons Kroy left over from the cabled sock in the previous chapter
3mm/US #2.5 needles for knitting
3.5mm/US #4 needle for binding off
2 stitch markers
Darning needle and several lengths of smooth, scrap yarn (or fishing line or unwaxed dental floss) for lifelines

GAUGE
The lace motif in the center should measure about 1¼ inches/3cm wide—don't worry too much.

METHOD

Using the long-tail method, cast on 13 sts.
Knit 3 rows.
Setup markers: K3, place marker, k7, place marker, k3.

Pattern section:
Use written or charted instructions, as you prefer.

Row 1 [RS]: Knit.
Row 2 [WS]: K3, p7, k3.
Feed a lifeline after this row.
Row 3 [RS]: K3, slip marker, k1, k2tog, yo, k1, yo, ssk, k1, slip marker, k3.
Row 4 [WS]: K3, p7, k3.
Row 5 [RS]: K3, slip marker, k2tog, yo, k3, yo, ssk, slip marker, k3.
Row 6 [WS]: K3, p7, k3.
Row 7 [RS]: K3, slip marker, k2, yo, s2kpo, yo, k2, slip marker, k3.
Row 8 [WS]: K3, p7, k3.

Repeat the last 8 rows 6 more times, for 7 full repeats.

Upper edge
Knit 5 rows. Bind off using the larger needle in your right hand.

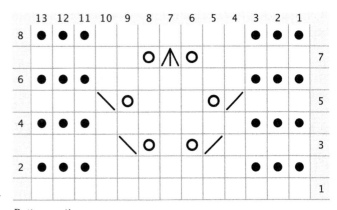

Pattern section

FINISHING

Soak in lukewarm water for 10 minutes. Roll in a towel to wring it out, and lay flat to dry. If you've got a place to do it, pin the four corners down and stretch it out. If not, once the piece is dry, iron it with a steam iron on a medium hot steam setting.

RECTANGULAR SCARF: CREST OF THE WAVE SCARF

(*As pictured on page 101*). Special Stitches used: Yo, ssk, k2tog

This scarf uses a classic Shetland pattern, the Crest of the Wave. It's much more than the sum of its parts—there's a single pattern row repeated four times, with a purled wrong side, and then there's four rows of garter stitch dividing up lacy sections.

The "double bias" created by the two directional sections—the first half of the motif leans to the right with two k2togs followed by the two compensating yarnovers, the second half of the motif leans to the left with two yarnovers followed by two compensatory ssk decreases—gives a lovely scalloped effect. This gives you a curvy upper and lower edge, but also causes the stripes in this variegated yarn to curve, too.

As with many other lace patterns, there's plenty of scope for substitution here. Choose about 225m of a worsted weight or heavier yarn, and use needles a size or two larger than those recommended on the ball band. It looks just as good in a solid color as it does in a variegated yarn.

FINISHED MEASUREMENTS

Approximately 6.5 inches wide and 60 inches long after blocking.

MATERIALS

1 skein variegated worsted or Aran weight yarn—sample used 1 skein Mountain Colors Yarns Mountain Goat (55% Mohair, 45% Wool, 230yds per 100gm) in color Copper Mountain
5mm/US #8 needles—straight or short circular, as you prefer
7mm/ US #10½ needle for binding off
6 stitch markers
Darning needle and several lengths of smooth, scrap yarn (or fishing line or unwaxed dental floss) for lifelines

GAUGE

Approximately 19 sts and 18 rows = 4 ins by 4 ins/10 cm by 10 cm in lace pattern using 5mm needles, blocked.
To check your gauge, cast on and work 2 repeats of the pattern. Slip the scarf to scrap yarn and block, pinning out the curves on the lower edge and along the top edge. Stretch vertically aggressively. Don't worry too much about matching the gauge precisely, as long as you like the fabric you are creating.

METHOD

Using the 5mm needle and the long tail method, cast on 39 sts.

Set up pattern and markers:
Rows 1–3: Knit.
Row 4 [RS]: K2, place marker, *k2tog twice, (yo, k1) 3 times, yo, ssk twice, place marker, k1; rep from * until 1 st remains, k1.
From here, slip markers as you come to them. They divide up the 11 sts of the pattern repeats, helping you keep count. For the first few rows, count your stitches after every lace pattern row. There are 4 rows of garter stitch between the patterned sections—if your stitch count is off, you can fix it in those garter rows with a k2tog or M1Z, as appropriate. If you're off by more than one stitch, I recommend pulling back to the most recent lifeline, just after the last garter section.

Row 5 [WS]: K2, p to last 2 sts, k2.
Rows 6, 8, 10 [RS]: K2, *k2tog twice, (yo, k1) 3 times, yo, ssk twice, k1; rep from * until 1 st remains, k1.
Rows 7, 9, 11 [WS]: K2, p to last 2 sts, k2.

Main pattern repeat:
Work from chart or written instructions, as you prefer.
Rows 1, 2, 3, 4: Knit.
Note: Thread a lifeline at this point.
Rows 5, 7, 9, 11 [RS]: K2, *k2tog twice, (yo, k1) 3 times, yo, ssk twice, k1; rep from * until 1 st remains, k1.
Rows 6, 8, 10, 12 [WS]: K2, p to last 2 sts, k2.

photo by Claude LaRue

Repeat the 12 rows of the main pattern repeat until you're almost out of yarn, *ending after a pattern row 3*. You can remove the lower lifelines as you work, or leave them all in place until you're done.

Using the 7mm needle, bind off.
Block by soaking scarf in lukewarm water, rolling in a towel to wring it out, and pin and leave flat to dry.

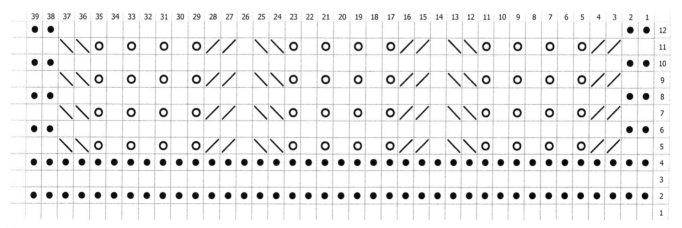

39	38	37	36	35	34	33	32	31	30	29	28	27	26	25	24	23	22	21	20	19	18	17	16	15	14	13	12	11	10	9	8	7	6	5	4	3	2	1	
•	•																																				•	•	12
		\	\	o		o		o		o	/	/		\	\	o		o		o		o	/	/		\	\	o		o		o		o	/	/			11
•	•																																				•	•	10
		\	\	o		o		o		o	/	/		\	\	o		o		o		o	/	/		\	\	o		o		o		o	/	/			9
•	•																																				•	•	8
		\	\	o		o		o		o	/	/		\	\	o		o		o		o	/	/		\	\	o		o		o		o	/	/			7
•	•																																				•	•	6
		\	\	o		o		o		o	/	/		\	\	o		o		o		o	/	/		\	\	o		o		o		o	/	/			5
•	•	•	•	•	•	•	•	•	•	•	•	•	•	•	•	•	•	•	•	•	•	•	•	•	•	•	•	•	•	•	•	•	•	•	•	•	•	•	4
																																							3
•	•	•	•	•	•	•	•	•	•	•	•	•	•	•	•	•	•	•	•	•	•	•	•	•	•	•	•	•	•	•	•	•	•	•	•	•	•	•	2
																																							1

Main pattern repeat

TIP-UP TRIANGLE: MODEST LACE SHAWL

(*As pictured on page 106*).Special Stitches used: Yo, ssk, k2tog, k3tog.
Other skills: tip up lace shawl shaping, adding repeats of a lace pattern.

This shawl is worked from the tip up to the top edge, starting with just 3 stitches.

Use markers liberally to divide up repeats of the lace pattern.

FINISHED MEASUREMENTS
After Blocking
Approximately 47 inches/120 cm wide.
Approximately 27 inches/70 cm from top edge to tip.

MATERIALS
3 x Debbie Bliss Baby Cashmerino (55% merino, 33% microfiber & 12% cashmere, 125m per 50gm ball), sample uses color 44
4.5mm/US #7 circular needle—16 inch/40cm or longer
Safety pin
Stitch markers—lots
Darning needle and several lengths of smooth, scrap yarn (or fishing line or unwaxed dental floss) for lifelines

GAUGE
21 sts and 28 rows over 4 inches/10 cm square in stockinette using 4.5mm circular needle.

PATTERN NOTES
Written Instructions for Lace Cable Panel
Row 1 [RS]: K2, k2tog, yo, k3.
Row 2 and all following even rows [WS]: Purl.
Row 3 [RS]: K1, k2tog, yo, k1, yo, ssk, k1.
Row 5 [RS]: K2tog, yo, k3, yo, ssk.
Row 7 [RS]: K2tog, yo, k2, k2tog, yo, k1.
Row 9 [RS]: K2, yo, k3tog, yo, k2.

METHOD
Lower edge
Cast on 3 stitches.
Row 1: Knit.
Row 2: K1, M1Z, k1, M1Z, k1.
Row 3: Knit.
Row 4: K1, M1Z, k3, M1Z, k1.
Row 5: K1, M1Z, k to last st, M1Z, k1.
Row 6: Knit.

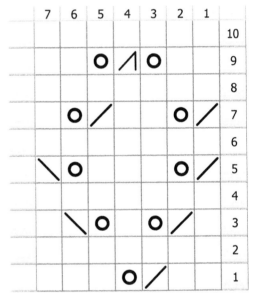

Lace Cable Panel

Repeat the last 2 rows until you've got 11 stitches on the needle.

Next row [RS]: K5, yo, k1, yo, k5. This is the right side—put a safety pin the fabric near the beginning of this row.
Following row [WS]: K5, p3, k5.

Set up first lace panel
Row 1 [RS]: K5, yo, k2tog, yo, k1, yo, k5.
Row 2 and all following even rows [WS]: K5, p to last 5 stitches, k5.
Row 3 [RS]: K5, yo, k2tog, yo, k1, yo, ssk, yo, k5.
Row 5 [RS]: K5, yo, k2tog, yo, k3, yo, ssk, yo, k5.
Row 7 [RS]: K5, yo, k1, pm, k2tog, yo, k2, k2tog, yo, k1, pm, k1, yo, k5.
Row 9 [RS]: K5, yo, knit to marker, k2, yo, k3tog, yo, k2, knit to last 5 stitches, yo, k5.
Row 10 [WS]: K5, p to last 5 stitches, k5.

Body

From here, you'll work as established:

RS rows: K5, yo, knit to first marker, work Lace Cable Panel, knit to last 5 stitches, yo, k5.

WS rows: K5, purl to last 5, k5.

Use either the written instructions or the chart for the lace cable panel, whichever you're more comfortable with.

The yarnovers just inside the garter edging at the start and end of the RS rows cause the shawl to widen.

When you've got 12 stitches outside the markers—5 for the garter edge and 7 in stockinette—you've got enough room to add another repeat of the lace pattern at each end. On the next RS row, work as follows: K5, yo, place marker; work lace pattern to last marker, work one more repeat of lace pattern, place another marker, yo, k5.

And then continue working. Note that when working these new lace repeats, just start the new ones on the same row you're working the existing repeats.

Feed a lifeline at least after every 20 rows –I recommend after every 10 rows as it gets wider.

Work until you have 21 repeats of the lace pattern across. End after R1 of the pattern repeat.

Work a WS row as normal.

Top edging

Work a plain right side row: K5, yo, knit to last 5 stitches, yo, k5. Work wrong side row as normal.

Work an eyelet row: K5, yo *k2tog, yo; repeat from * to last 6 stitches, k1, yo, k5.

Work 6 rows garter stitch—that is, knitting all the way across, no increases.

With wrong side row facing, work the purl version of the Russian Lace bind off as follows:

P2, *slip these two stitches back onto the left needle, p2tog, p1; repeat from * until a single stitch remains. Break yarn and pull the end through to secure.

This bind off has plenty of stretch, to accommodate the blocking.

FINISHING

Soak the shawl in lukewarm water with a little wool wash for about 15 minutes. Roll in a towel to wring it out. Stretch and pin out the three corners of the shawl—to blocking mats, onto towels on a low-pile carpet, or use clothes pegs to secure to your laundry rack. Let dry.

TOP-DOWN TRIANGLE: SPRING LEAVES

(*As pictured on page 106*). This triangular shawl starts at the top, in contrast to the previous shawl. The geometry of this is different because of the placement of the increases. There are four increases in every right side row: one each at the start and end of the row, and two in the middle. Those two increases at the edges cause the shawl to widen; the two increases in the middle of the row cause the stitches to be pushed out to the sides. You can spot a triangle that's worked top-down because the rows bend—there is a right angle along the center spine. In the previous triangle, the rows are straight across.

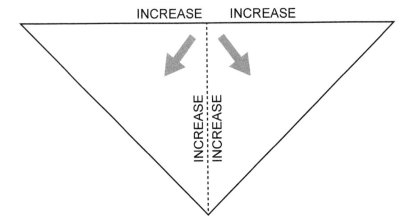

Top-down shawl shaping

This shaping makes for a triangle that's wider than it is deep.

This pattern doesn't lend itself to the use of markers, but a small repeat—only 6 stitches and 6 rows—keeps it pretty simple. It's all about keeping the motifs lined up. Use lifelines liberally!

FINISHED MEASUREMENTS
After Blocking:
Approximately 60 inches/150 cm wide.
Approximately 30 inches/75cm from top edge to tip.

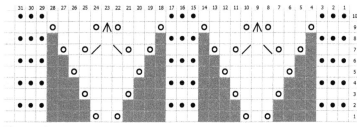
Chart 1: Start

MATERIALS
1 skein Classic Elite Alpaca Sox (60% alpaca, 20% merino, 20% nylon, 450yds per 100gm skein), Sample uses color 1874. An equivalent length of any sock yarn will work nicely for this pattern. I like an alpaca blend as it blooms beautifully when blocked.
4mm/US #6 circular needle—16 inch/40cm or longer
Darning needle and several lengths of smooth, scrap yarn (or fishing line or unwaxed dental floss) for lifelines

GAUGE
Approximately 16 sts and 26 rows = 4 ins by 4 ins/10 cm by 10 cm in lace pattern using 4mm needle.

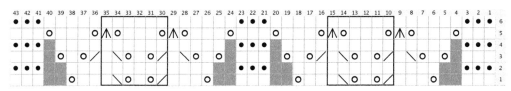
Chart 2: Body

METHOD
Using the long-tail method, cast on 11 stitches.
Establish border: Knit 5 rows.

Starting pattern:
Row 1 [RS]: Work chart 1 row 1 across all sts. 15 sts.

Row 2 [WS]: Work chart 1 row 2 across all sts.
Row 3 [RS]: Work chart 1 row 3 across all sts.
Continue until chart 1 row 10 is complete. You should have 31 sts.

Feed a lifeline at this point.

Body of shawl
Row 1 [RS]: Work chart 2 row 1 across all sts.
Row 2 [WS]: Work chart2 row 2 across all sts.

Continue working chart 2. Pay attention to the repeat indicated in the central sections of the shawl. After every 6 rows of the chart, your shawl will have gained 12 stitches—6 on each side of the central spine. Those 6 new stitches add another repeat of the 6-stitch pattern in those side sections. The first time through the 6 rows, you'll only work that 6-stitch repeat once. The second time through the 6 rows, you'll work the 6-stitch repeat twice; the third time, you'll work the 6-stitch repeat three times—and so forth. The 6-stitch repeat is marked off in the chart with a heavy border.

Feed lifelines as you go—every 12 rows or so.

Work chart 2 until you've got 21 leaf motifs on each side, ending after a Row 6.

Establish lower edging:
Before proceeding, feed a lifeline.
Work Chart 3, paying attention to the 6-stitch repeat (marked as before with a heavy border) to be worked in the side sections.
Continue until all chart rows are complete.

KNITTERLY ADVICE

Place a stitch marker between each lace repeat as you're working, and do it proudly. It's not a crutch — it frees your brain to be able to concentrate on the lace stitches, rather than where you are in the repeat sequence.

— Amy R. Singer, knitty.com

Bind off as follows:
With WS facing, work a Russian Lace Bind off as follows:

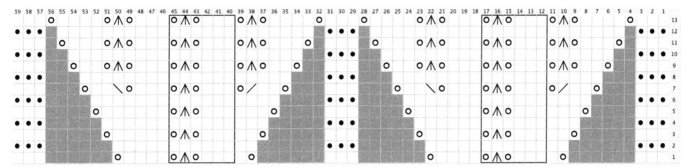

Chart 3: Edging

K2, *insert tip of left needle into the fronts of these stitches as if to ssk, and knit these two stitches together, k1; repeat from * until a single stitch remains. Break yarn and pull the end through to secure.
This is a variation of the bind off used in the previous shawl pattern. It has a slightly lower profile, but a little less stretch.

FINISHING
Soak the shawl in lukewarm water with a little woolwash for about 15 minutes. Roll in a towel to wring it out. Stretch and pin out the three corners of the shawl—to blocking mats, onto towels on a low-pile carpet, or use clothes pegs to secure to your laundry rack. If you've got rustproof pins, pin out the scallops of the edging. Let dry.

Weave in ends.

WHAT'S NEXT

As with cables, explore more complex combinations! Take a look through some stitch libraries to see what sorts of amazing patterns you can build from these basic building blocks:
The Barbara Walker Stitch Treasuries are fabulous; and volume 5 in the *Vogue Stitchionary* Series is entirely focused on lace.

For lace patterns, look for the books *Lace Style* by Pam Allen, *Folk Shawls* by Cheryl Oberle, *A Gathering of Lace* by Meg Swansen, and *Victorian Lace Today* by Jane Sowerby.

Lace Style has a broad range of patterns—scarves and garments—of varying degrees of difficulty. The other books are focused on scarves and shawls, many of them very traditional in style and patterning. There's patterns of all levels of difficulty in these books—a few entry level pieces accessible even to the newest knitters, and designs that will challenge and engage even the most experienced knitter.

KNITTERLY ADVICE

Practice safe lace — always use a lifeline!.

— Vicki Norton, knitter

Chapter 11: Colorwork

INTRODUCTION

Color is the easiest way to customize your knitting—whether it's just knitting a pattern in a different color than the one used for the sample, or getting creative with stripes and color changes.

It's also a great way to use up leftovers. If you don't have enough yarn to complete the project, a second color can be a great help! If you're working a hat or mittens or socks or something with a well-defined edging, work the edging(s) in one color, and the rest of the piece in the main color.

A simple hat looks completely different with a simple change of color after the ribbing.

A pair of basic socks becomes something wonderful if you use a different color to work the ribbing, the heel and the toe.

And of course using multiple colors in a Fair Isle pattern results in some of the most beautiful knitting you can create.

If you're not choosing precisely the same brand and weight of yarn, it's a good idea to choose yarns in the same gauge and with the same washability characteristics. I made a pair of striped socks once with two yarns from my stash. One was machine washable, the other wasn't—which of course I only discovered after I washed them the first time.

SKILLS TAUGHT

Stripes, Fair Isle; one-handed and two-handed stranding, intarsia, reading colorwork charts. Corrugated ribbing, i-cord and applied i-cord

STRIPES

Stripes are very straightforward: you just drop the old color and start working with the new one! There are a few things to keep in mind to help keep it easy and fun.

How to join the new color: leaving a four or five inch tail, tie the new color onto the old color; a simple overhand knot will do it. The knot isn't about permanence, it's about positioning. Start the next row with the new color—simple. The knot will keep the two yarns together, and ensure that the last stitch of the old color and the first stitch of the new color are even and tight.

TO CUT OR NOT TO CUT?

If you're alternating two colors, you need to decide whether you have to cut the ends each time you change, or if you can carry the unused yarn. If your stripes are short—no more than four rows—just let the unused yarn hang at the side, and pick it up again when you need it. If your stripes take more than four rows, cut the yarn and join it as if you're joining a new ball. If you carry a strand too far up the side, you risk pulling and puckering the side of your work.

If the edge is going to be exposed—for example, in a scarf or a blanket, twist the two strands around each other when you're at that end of the row. This ensures the unused yarn snugs up to the edge and hides.

When working back and forth (that is, not in the round) stripes are most often worked in even numbers—that way, you can carry the yarn up the side between stripes. One row stripes require you to cut the yarn each time when you change—annoying!

STRIPES IN THE ROUND

Of course if you're working stripes in the round, a single row stripe works fine. There is another quirk about working stripes in the round, however: the jog. If you're working in the round, you're actually working in spirals so that the start and end of a given round are staggered. You can't see this when working in a solid color, but it becomes visible when you change colors. It's actually visible even in commercially made socks:

When I first noticed it, I'll be honest: I panicked. I thought I'd done something wrong. Nope! It's just the way it is. If I am working a striped item in the round, I'll arrange it so that the round change is less obvious—for a hat, I'll position it at the back. For socks, I'll position the start of round at the back of the leg, and in the center of the sole. (See "What's Next" on page 123 for more on this).

Tying on new yarn

FAIR ISLE

There are two types of knitting that are considered to be "formal" colorwork: Fair Isle and Intarsia.

The term Fair Isle, named after the Scottish island, is used to describe any knitting where two colors are used across a row (or round).

For example, the two pairs of socks in the photo at left are both worked in Fair Isle.

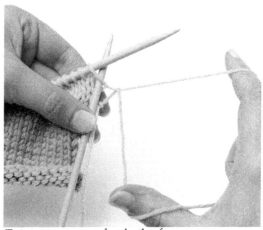
Twisting yarns around each other for a carry

In both these cases, the socks are knitted with two colors, and both colors are used across the entire round. You alternate strands as you work, a few stitches in one color, a few stitches in the next, and so forth. The unused strand lies across the back of the knitting, waiting until you need it again.

Fair Isle knitting is beautiful but also very practical: it makes very warm mittens and socks. The unused strands at the back—known as the floats—form a layer of insulation.

Pulling green over yellow

WORKING FAIR ISLE

Part of the beauty and cleverness of Fair Isle is that it looks significantly more complicated than it is: no matter how many colors in a given project, only two are ever used in a row.

Pulling yellow from under the green

And those colors are alternated frequently—typically there's no more than 5 or 6 stitches in one color at a time—to help you to keep even gauge.

The trick with working Fair Isle is to not tangle the yarns. Keep them as separate as you can.

(Note that there are some books that tell you that if you're working with two different colors you're supposed to twist them around each other when you change. This isn't always true, and when working Fair Isle, doing it will make your life miserable by making your knitting too tight and getting you in a horrible tangle.)

To keep yourself sane, keep your yarns separate, as follows: Designate an "upper" and a "lower" yarn for your row. I will often decide based on which color is designated at the main color in the pattern—main color upper, contrast color lower. If there isn't a specific MC and CC, I will arrange them in alphabetical order; if using red and blue, blue is my upper yarn, red is my lower yarn.

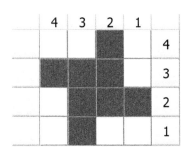

Fair Isle after blocking

If I'm following the houndstooth chart in green and yellow, I will work as follows:

Cast on a multiple of 4 sts, 16 for example, in the main color, the green. At the start of the first row join the contrasting color, the yellow, by tying it on. The green is my MC so it will be my upper color; the yellow will be my lower color.

Knit two stitches normally in the green (working either English or Continental style, doesn't matter). Drop the yarn. When picking up the yellow strand, pull it from underneath the green, keeping it below the green strand.

Knit one stitch with the yellow, and then drop the yarn.

When picking up the green strand, pull it over the yellow; keeping the green strand above the yellow strand.

Knit three with the green, and change back to the yellow, pulling it from under the green… and so forth.

When changing colors, don't pull too tight. I know, I know: this sounds glib. Do your best to leave the floats reasonably relaxed. If you've got a long stretch of one color, wrap the new color around your finger when changing.

No matter how skilled you are, your Fair Isle knitting will be less smooth and tighter than your single-color knitting. Stranding reduces the stretch of a fabric—the strands limit the movement and the floats cause the fabric to pull in. Even the best knitter will have a different gauge in a stranded pattern than working plain.

For example, my purple and black patterned socks are worked in a sock yarn I've used often; when working plain in that yarn, I need just 56 stitches; in the colorwork pattern, I needed 70 stitches to make a sock that fits me.

It is true that dropping and picking up the strands each time you change color is slow and cumbersome, but it's a good way to start and get familiar with the stranding process. The objective is to minimize the number of times the yarns get twisted around each other; the process outlined here lets them overlap in a regularized fashion, keeping them tidy, reasonably close and flat to the fabric, while still gently "locking" the stiches in so you don't have huge gaps between the colors.

Once you get the hang of it, you can keep hold of both strands as you work: You can work with two colors two different ways: with both strands in the same hand, or one in each hand. If you knit English style, practice carrying both yarns in your right hand Everyone will develop their own style, but I tend to wrap one strand with my index finger while carrying the other inelegantly but effectively with my thumb.

If you knit Continental, you can carry both yarns on different fingers in your left hand. "Pick" the first yarn normally, and then when "picking" for the second strand, just poke the needle over top of the first strand.

If you're ambidextrous, or just plain good with both techniques, carry one strand in one hand, and one strand in the other, and work the one yarn English style, and the other Continental style. This is the fastest method and it's worth trying as it often solves problems with tension. In fact, although I'm predominantly an English-style knitter, I learned to knit Continental style precisely for this reason: to improve my colorwork.

No matter which hand they're in, carrying both yarns at the same time helps you keep them separate, since they won't cross in your hands.

The key to successful Fair Isle knitting is to remember that however you handle the two yarns—dropping and picking them up individually, or keeping in them in the same hand or in separate hands—just keep them separate as much as possible. If they do twist around each other, untwist them periodically.

FAIR ISLE PATTERNS

As with the houndstooth example above, Fair Isle patterns are most often charted—colorwork is a very visual activity, and the instructions are best expressed visually.

The majority of Fair Isle designs are worked in the round, as it is significantly easier to do colorwork on the knit side than it is on the purl side for two reasons: handling two yarns is fiddlier on the purl side, and it's harder to "read" the knitting from the back. When working color patterns, knitters tend to use previous rows as a guide to make sure they are working correctly. You can easily confirm that your patterning is lined up by comparing the right side of your knitting to the chart. It's hard to look at it on the wrong side, as the floats hide the stitches.

It's so much easier to work Fair Isle in the round that many knitters prefer to knit even cardigans in the round, and then cut the knitting when it's done! This is known as steeking. It's a technique commonly used in Scandinavian sweaters—look closely at those gorgeous Scandinavian cardigans—they all have ribbon at the front edges, obscuring the cut. The edges are sewn (most often by machine) before they are cut, so the knitting doesn't unravel.

Fair Isle is typically worked with pure wool (or other animal fibers) as it requires blocking to make it look its best, and of all the fibers, wool responds best to blocking. No matter how good a knitter you are, Fair Isle is always uneven and bumpy when it comes off your needles. Blocking evens everything out, and smooths the surface of your knitting. For Fair Isle, I recommend not only soaking and laying flat to dry, but a good blast from a steamer or steam iron really helps, too.

Fair Isle that will be steeked should be worked in a felting (i.e. non-machine-washable) wool so that the edges felt together a little bit for more security.

INTARSIA

Intarsia, simply defined, is blobs of color. Intarsia knitting differs from Fair Isle in that you don't carry the colors all the way across the row.

Vertical stripes are the simplest example of intarsia. One side of the swatch shown here is worked in green, the other side in yellow, in distinct blocks.

This is where you *do* want to twist the yarns around each other. If you were to just drop the one color in the middle of the row, and start knitting with the other, you'd have two separate, unjoined pieces of knitting:

So when you drop the one color, twist the new one around it, like so, just as you would for carrying the yarn up the side of a striped scarf, in fact.

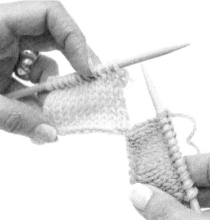

Intarsia without twist

You can see at the back of the swatch the two pieces are "woven" together:

The classic use of intarsia is the "Mary Maxim" sweater, so known as they were popularized in North America by the Canadian yarn company Mary Maxim in the 1950s and 1960s. The motifs are big blobs of color, worked in sections across a row.

And in another contrast to Fair Isle, intarsia is most easily worked flat. (If you're working a block of 10 stitches in one color, you need the yarn to be positioned at the start of the block when working the next row. When going back and forth in rows, the yarn is in the right place. When working in the round, the yarn will end up at the wrong end of the block.) As with Fair Isle, intarsia patterns are also typically charted.

Twisting at the color change

Working intarsia is straightforward in that you are only ever working with one yarn at a time—when changing yarns in a row you drop the old and pick up the new, twist one around the other, and keep knitting. Where it gets more challenging is that depending on the complexity of the pattern, you can have more than two balls attached to your row.

I won't lie: intarsia is very divisive. Some knitters love it, other knitters find it too tangly and hard to manage. It's a very personal choice. Once you've got the hang of Fair Isle, give it a go and see what you think!

Back side of intarsia piece

WORKING WITH COLOR: PICK WHAT YOU LOVE

When combining colors for a project, or when looking at heaps of leftovers, many knitters feel nervous about how to put them together. When I was just starting out as a knitter, I had only ever studied color theory in high-school art classes. I felt like I knew just enough about color to feel totally unqualified. I was nervous about choosing two colors for stripes, as I wasn't sure they would "go together." I wasn't even sure what it meant for colors to "go together."

The more I knit, the braver I became: just try it! The trick is to knit with the colors you love. Let the colors you see around you inspire you: your favorite flowers, your favorite stripy t-shirt, the colors of your calico cat.

Don't let an art teacher scare you; don't worry about hue or intensity or value or the color wheel. Pick what appeals to you. I love orange, and I especially love it in stripes with black, and white, and blue and red and even pink. An interior designer may not approve, but I love the knitting that results. You are your own designer—knit with what makes you happy.

TWO OR THREE OR FIFTY

If, however, you feel better having some guidelines when you are adding color to a project, the following can help produce a result that's more pleasing. Choose two colors you like and alternate them. If you happen to remember a little color theory from your art class, then choose three complementary colors. Or choose a million colors and don't worry about it. The more colors in a project, the less you need to worry about theory and correctness and matchiness.

For example, this vest is knitted using yarn leftover from a blanket project. The yarn is Noro Kureyon, and I had bits and pieces from about 25 different balls. I didn't worry about whether the next stripe matched the previous one, I just let the colors fall where they may. And the result is insane and bright and wonderful, while breaking every rule in the art school book.

The designer Kaffe Fassett is the undisputed master of the "more is more" school of color: check out not only his knitting books, but his quilting and patchwork books, too—they're a great source of inspiration.

WHEN NOT TO USE COLOR

Lots of color isn't always a good idea. If your project has many pattern stitches—cables or lace for example—too much color can obscure all your hard work. And a dark color can be a bad choice, too. I have knitted cabled sweaters in black, but they're pretty hard to see. No matter how many and which colors you're working with, enjoy it!

MINI PROJECT: PHONE COZY

Colorwork is most easily worked in the round, and this little phone cozy gives you an ideal place to practice. I used a bright yellow to ensure I could easily find my phone in my bag.

Other skills: colorwork from a chart.

FINISHED MEASUREMENTS

Approximately 5.5 inches around and 4.5 inches tall. Fits iPhone and other similarly shaped phones and devices. The cozy should be a little bit smaller than the phone so it fits snugly.

MATERIALS

Scraps of worsted weight yarn—I used less than 20gm each of two colors of leftover Cascade 220 in colors 7827 (bright yellow) as MC and 8555 (black) as CC.

4.5mm/US #7 double-pointed needles

GAUGE

22 sts and 28 ridges = 4 ins by 4 ins/10 cm by 10 cm in Fair Isle pattern in the round. You don't need to check your gauge before you start, but partway through the project you should check to make sure you're getting something close.

Remember that your gauge in Fair Isle will be tighter than if the yarn is worked plain on the same size needles.

METHOD

Using the long-tail method and MC, cast on 30 stitches onto a single needle. Distribute across three needles as evenly as possible, and join for working in the round. Remember that you are at the start of the round when your working yarn and the yarn tail from the cast on are lined up.

Setup round: K15, m1, k15.

Round 1: Work chart row 1 around.

Round 2: Work chart row 2 around.

Round 3: Join CC and work chart row 3 around.

Legend:

☐	**MC**
■	**CC**
▨	**No Stitch**
╱	**k2tog**

Continue working chart until all rows are complete, taking care to work decrease as indicated in final round.

Ribbing round: (K1, p1) around.
Repeat Ribbing round 7 more times. Bind off in ribbing.

FINISHING
Using horizontal seam method (page 89) seam lower edge. Weave in ends. Wash.

CANDY CANE CHRISTMAS STOCKING

Other skills: i-cord and applied i-cord

This stocking is knit at a slightly tighter than usual gauge for this yarn to ensure a nice dense fabric to hold all those gifts. The stitch pattern is brilliantly simple—no chart needed. You just alternate 2 stitches in red and 2 stitches in white, and because there's an odd number of stitches, the patterning just wraps around the leg.

The i-cord technique is used to create the loop and the edging around the top.

FINISHED MEASUREMENTS
Approximately 15 inches long from cuff to bottom of foot, and 12 inches long from toe to back of heel.

MATERIALS
1 ball Brown Sheep Lamb's Pride Superwash Worsted (100% wool, 220 yds per 100g ball). Sample uses color SW01 Red Wing.
1 ball Lamb's Pride Superwash Worsted. Sample uses color SW11 White Frost.
Any equivalent worsted weight yarn will do—e.g. Cascade 220.
4mm (US#6) 16-inch circular needle
1 set 4mm (US#6) double-pointed needles
stitch marker

GAUGE
24 sts and 24 rows = 4 ins by 4 ins/10 cm by 10 cm in the round in Fair Isle pattern.

TECHNIQUES AND PATTERN NOTES
Wrap and turn:
On the knit side, slip the next stitch purlwise; bring the yarn to the front, and slip the stitch back to the left needle. Move the yarn to the back again and turn the knitting around so that the wrong side is facing.
On the purl side, slip the next stitch purlwise; move the yarn to the back, and slip the stitch back to the left needle. Bring the yarn to the front again and turn the knitting around so that the right side is facing.

Working the wrapped stitches together with the wraps:
On the knit side, insert the right hand needle under the wrap(s), and knit it (them) together with the stitch.
On the purl side, insert the right hand needle under the wrap(s) on the right side of of your knitting (that is, the side that is facing away from you), and pull it up onto the left hand needle. Purl the wrap(s) together with the stitch.

METHOD
Leg:
With red, and using the circular needle, cast on 75 sts. Place a marker for the start of the round and join for working in the round, being careful not to twist. Join white yarn.
Fair Isle pattern: *K2 with red, k2 with white; repeat.
After the first round, don't forget to check to see if your knitting is twisted.

Work Fair Isle pattern around leg. Since there's an uneven number of sts in the round, the Fair Isle pattern will wrap cleverly around the leg. Leave the marker for start of round in place, but just slip it as you work around and keep the pattern going. Continue until leg measures 11 inches from cast-on edge.

Work to end of current round, and take note of where you are in the Fair Isle pattern when you stop. You will need to pick up the pattern again after you've turned the heel.

Turn heel:
You'll work the heel in short rows, back and forth. Drop—don't cut!—the white, and continue only with the red.

Heel step 1, row 1 [RS]: K35, wrap and turn.
Heel step 1, row 2 [WS]: P34, wrap and turn.
Heel step 1, row 3 [RS]: K33, wrap and turn.
Heel step 1, row 4 [WS]: P32, wrap and turn.

Continue as established, working one stitch fewer every row (that is, to one stitch before previously wrapped stitch) until 12 sts remain unwrapped in the middle. RS should be facing for next row.

Heel step 2, row 1 [RS]: Knit to first wrapped stitch, knit this stitch together with its wrap, wrap and turn next stitch. This stitch will have a double wrap.
Heel step 2, row 2 [WS]: Purl to first wrapped stitch, purl this stitch together with its wrap, wrap and turn next stitch.
Heel step 2, row 3 [RS]: Knit to first double wrapped stitch, knit this stitch together with its two wraps, wrap and turn.
Heel step 2, row 4 [WS]: Purl to first wrapped stitch, purl this stitch together with its two wraps, wrap and turn.

Repeat Heel step 2 rows 3 and 4 until all double-wrapped sts have been worked. RS will be facing, and you will be where you left off with the leg. If you removed the start of round marker when working the heel, put it back at this position.

Foot:
Working again with both yarns, continue Fair Isle pattern where you left off and work across heel sts, and around the instep sts to reunite the round.

Note: You may find that there are small gaps or holes at the edges of the heel. You can close those up by picking up a strand of yarn in the gap (as per an M1L, page 42) and working it together with the next stitch.

Work even in pattern until foot measures approximately 9 inches from back of heel. On final round, place a second marker after stitch 37, or divide the stitches up so that the first 37 sts are grouped together, and the remaining 38 are grouped together. The first 37 sts are the sole sts, the rem 38 are the instep sts.

Cut white yarn, leaving a 4 inch tail. From here, you'll work only in red.
Toe decrease round: K1, ssk, knit to 3 sts before end of sole sts (that is, 3 sts before the first marker), k2tog, k2, ssk, knit to 3 sts before end of round, k2tog, k1.
Next round: Knit.
Repeat the above two rounds 7 more times, 43 sts rem.
Work the decrease round only 8 times until 11 sts rem.
Cut yarn, leaving a 6 inch tail. With a yarn needle, thread the tail through the final sts and pull to close.

Top Edging & Hook:
Using red yarn and a circular needle, cast on 3 sts. With those three sts on the needle on the right hand tip of the needle, starting at center back of leg with RS facing, pick up 50 sts around cast-on edge at top of leg. Don't join.
With a single double-pointed needle, starting with the three cast-on stitches, work applied i-cord edge as follows:
Knit 2, ssk. (The ssk is worked with the last of the cast-on stitches and the first picked up stitch around the top of the stocking.)
Don't turn the double-pointed needle, but slide the three sts just worked back to the beginning of the needle they are on, so that you're in position to knit them again. Pull the yarn tight so that it crosses across the back of the three sts to form a cord, and repeat the applied i-cord row.
Work until all 50 sts of the top edging have been decreased, and 3 sts total remain.

Work i-cord as follows on those three sts:
K3. Slide the three sts just worked back to the beginning of the needle, and pull the yarn across the back of the row.

Repeat until i-cord extension measures approximately 6 inches. Bind off.
Sew end of i-cord down beside the start, to form a loop.

Wash to block and even out the stitches, and weave in all ends to finish.

ZIG ZAG FAIR ISLE TAM

(*As shown on page 119.*) Other skills: corrugated ribbing, i-cord

A tam is a classic colorwork project—the top of the hat makes an ideal canvas for fun color and stitch patterns.

My good friend Natalie Selles designed this hat for me. She's a wizard with colorwork and Fair Isle hats are her specialty.

The decreases are worked in such a way as to not interrupt the patterning—very clever!

FINISHED MEASUREMENTS
Small: 16.75 inches around band; Medium: 19.25 inches around band; Large: 21.5 inches around band.
Choose a size a couple of inches smaller than your head circumference.

MATERIALS
1 (1, 2) Knit Picks Wool of the Andes (100% Peruvian Highland Wool, 110yds per 50gm ball) in MC; sample uses color 24076, Onyx Heather
1 (1, 1) Knit Picks Wool of the Andes (100% Peruvian Highland Wool, 110yds per 50gm ball in CC1; sample uses color 25068, Wonderland Heather
1 (1, 1) Knit Picks Wool of the Andes (100% Peruvian Highland Wool, 110yds per 50gm ball in CC2; sample uses color 23899, Sapphire Heather
16 inch (40cm) 4.5mm (US#7) circular needle
16 inch (40cm) 5mm (US#8) circular needle
1 set 5mm (US#8) double-pointed needles
stitch marker

GAUGE
20 sts and 24 rounds = 4 ins by 4 ins/10 cm by 10 cm in the round in Fair Isle pattern.

METHOD
Using MC and smaller circular needle with the long tail method, cast on 84 (96, 108) sts.

Join CC1.
Corrugated ribbing round: (K2 with MC, p2 with CC1) to end of round. To work corrugated ribbing, start with both yarns at the back. To work the p2, bring the CC1 yarn to the front, purl the 2 stitches, and then move the yarn to back, before changing to the MC for the k2. Repeat corrugated ribbing round 7 times more.

Change to larger circular needle and work an increase round: Using MC only (k2, m1) to end of round. I recommend the M1Z here. 126 (144, 162) sts.

Join CC2.
Round 1: With both MC and CC2, work Chart A row 1 around.
Round 2: With both MC and CC2, work Chart A row 2 around.
Round 3: With both MC and CC2, work Chart A row 3 around.
Round 4: With both MC and CC2, work Chart A row 4 around.
Round 5: With MC only, knit around.

6	5	4	3	2	1	
					◆	4
◆				◆		3
	◆		◆			2
		◆				1

Zig zag chart A

6	5	4	3	2	1	
		■				4
	■		■			3
■				■		2
					■	1

Zig zag chart B

Legend
☐ MC
■ CC1
◆ CC2

Round 6: With both MC and CC1, work Chart B row 1 around.
Round 7: With both MC and CC1, work Chart B row 2 around.
Round 8: With both MC and CC1, work Chart B row 3 around.
Round 9: With both MC and CC1, work Chart B row 4 around.
Round 10: With MC only, knit around.
Repeat Rounds 1–10 once more, and Rounds 1–4 once more.

Crown round 1: With MC only, (k1, k2tog) around. 84 (96, 108) sts.
Crown round 2: With both MC and CC1, work Chart B row 1 around.
Crown round 3: With both MC and CC1, work Chart B row 2 around.
Crown round 4: With both MC and CC1, work Chart B row 3 around.
Crown round 5: With both MC and CC1, work Chart B row 4 around.
Change to double-pointed needles.
Crown round 6: With MC only k2tog around. 42 (48, 54) sts.
Crown round 7: With both MC and CC2, work Chart A row 1 around.
Crown round 8: With both MC and CC2, work Chart A row 2 around.
Crown round 9: With both MC and CC2, work Chart A row 3 around.
Crown round 10: With both MC and CC2, work Chart A row 4 around.
Crown round 11: With MC only, k2tog around. 21 (24, 27) sts.

Cut both CC1 and CC2.

With MC only, finish as follows:
Crown round 12: Knit around.
Crown round 13: K2tog 10 (12, 13) times, k 1 (0, 1). 11 (12, 14) sts.
Crown round 14: Knit around.
Crown round 15: K2tog 5 (6, 7) times, k1 (0, 0). 6 (6, 7) sts.
Crown round 16: K2tog 3 times, k 0 (0, 1). 3 (3, 4) sts.
Size L only, Crown round 17: K1, k2tog, k1. –(–, 3) sts.

Work i-cord as follows:
Row 1: K3.
Slip sts back to beginning of needle (with RS facing), and repeat Row 1 again. Pull yarn tight across the back to form cord.
Repeat this twice more.

Break yarn and pull through 3 sts to finish off. Weave in ends.

To block: soak the hat in lukewarm water and roll in a towel to wring out most of the moisture. Stretch the hat over a dinner plate that is 12–13 inches in diameter and leave to dry.

HOUNDSTOOTH SOCKS

(*As shown on page 121.*) Special techniques: Three-needle bind off.

This is the most challenging pattern in the book—but it's worth it.

The stitch pattern is actually quite straightforward—the challenging part comes when working the gusset and toe decreases. You need to pay attention to keep the stripes lined up. It's all written out, so as long as you are able to focus (that is, this ain't no TV knitting), you'll be fine.

FINISHED SIZES
Women's S—fits up shoe size 6½, Women's M—fits shoe sizes 7–9, Women's L—fits shoe sizes 9½+. For wider feet, work a larger size and adjust the foot length as required.

MATERIALS
1 x 100gm skein Fortissima Sock 100 sock yarn (457 yds per skein, 75% superwash wool, 25% nylon). Sample uses color 2002 (black) as MC.
1 x 100gm skein Fortissima Sock 100 sock yarn (457 yds per skein, 75% superwash wool, 25% nylon). Sample uses color 2024 (brilliant

white) as CC.

1 set 2.5mm (US #1.5) double pointed needles or a 32 inch/80 cm or longer 2.5mm circular needle for magic loop method

stitch holder

5 stitch markers: 2 of one color (marker A), 2 of a second color (marker B), 1 of a third color (marker C)

length of smooth, contrasting color scrap yarn

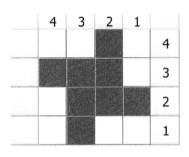

Houndstooth Chart. As noted in the Materials list, black is the MC and white is the CC in the socks pictured here, but you can use any two colors you like. Just make sure you use them consistently, i.e. color #1 is always MC and color #2 is always CC.

GAUGE

40 stitches and 46 rounds = 4 inches/10 cm in stranded Fair-Isle Houndstooth pattern in the round, after blocking

METHOD

Using MC and the long tail method, cast on 72 (80, 88) stitches. Note or mark beginning of round and distribute stitches across your needles as you prefer and join for working in the round, being careful not to twist. I recommend having a multiple of four stitches on each needle.

Corrugated Ribbing round: *K1 MC, p1 CC; rep from * to end of round.
Repeat Corrugated Ribbing round until sock measures 1 inch from cast on.

Leg round 1: Work Houndstooth Chart row 1 18 (20, 22) times across round.
Leg round 2: Work Houndstooth Chart row 2 18 (20, 22) times across round.
Continue as established until leg measures 6 (6.5, 7) ins from cast on, ending with a Row 4 of Houndstooth Chart.

Divide for heel:
This portion is worked both and forth in rows in a vertical stripe pattern across first 36 (40, 44) sts of round.
Heel row 1 [RS]: (K1 MC, k1 CC) 18 (20, 22) times, turn.
Heel row 2 [WS]: Sl 1, p1 MC, (p1 CC, p1 MC) 17 (19, 21) times, turn.
Heel row 3 [RS]: Sl 1, k1 CC, (k1 MC, k1 CC) 17 (19, 21) times, turn.
Heel row 4 [WS]: Sl 1, p1 MC, (p1 CC, p1 MC) 17 (19, 21) times, turn.
Repeat rows 3 & 4 another 9 (10, 11) times—22 (24, 26) rows total in heel flap.

Turn heel, size Small:
Continuing only on heel stitches, work as follows:
Heel Row 1 [RS]: (K1 MC, k1 CC) 12 (–, –) times, ssk with MC, turn.
Heel Row 2 [WS]: Slip 1, (p1 CC, p1 MC) 6 (–, –) times, p2tog with CC, turn.
Heel Row 3 [RS]: Slip 1, (k1 CC, k1 MC) 6 (–, –) times, ssk with MC, turn.
Heel Row 4 [WS]: Slip 1, (p1 CC, p1 MC) 6 (–, –) times, p2tog with CC, turn.
Repeat Rows 3 & 4 until 14 (–, –) stitches rem, and RS is facing for next row.

Turn heel, sizes Medium & Large:
Continuing only on heel stitches, work as follows:
Heel Row 1 [RS]: (K1 MC, k1 CC) – (13, 14) times, k1 MC, ssk with CC, turn.
Heel Row 2 [WS]: Slip 1, (p1 MC, p1 CC) – (7, 7) times, p2tog with MC, turn.
Heel Row 3 [RS]: Slip 1, (k1 CC, k1 MC) – (7, 7) times, ssk with CC, turn.
Heel Row 4 [WS]: Slip 1, (p1 MC, p1 CC) – (7, 7) times, p2tog MC, turn.
Repeat Rows 3 & 4 until – (16, 16) stitches rem, and RS is facing for next row.

Rejoin round and set up gusset:
Work across 14 (16, 16) stitches of heel in stripe pattern as established.

Size Small: Pick up and knit 16 (–, –) stitches for gussets along the first side of the heel flap as follows: (pick up and knit 1 CC), (pick up and knit 1 MC, 3 CC) twice, (pick up and knit 1 MC, 1 CC) three times, pick up and knit 1 MC, place marker A for start of instep stitches; work across instep stitches in pattern as per Houndstooth Chart row 1; place second marker A for end of instep stitches; along the second side of the heel flap (pick up and knit 1 MC, 1 CC) three times, pick up and knit 1 CC, (1 MC, 3 CC) twice, pick up and knit 1 MC; place marker C for new start of round.

Size Medium: Pick up and knit – (17, –) stitches for gussets along the first side of the heel flap as follows: (pick up and knit 2 CC), (pick up and knit 1 MC, 3 CC) twice, (pick up and knit 1 MC, 1 CC) 3 times, pick up and knit 1 MC, place marker A for start of instep stitches; work across instep stitches in pattern as per Houndstooth Chart row 1, starting the first repeat at st 2 of the chart; place second marker A for end of instep stitches; along the second side of the heel flap (pick up and knit 1 MC, 1 CC) three times, pick up and knit 1 CC, (1 MC, 3 CC) twice, pick up and knit (1 MC, 1 CC); place marker C for new start of round.

Size Large: Pick up and knit – (–, 19) stitches for gussets along the first side of the heel flap as follows: (pick up and knit 1 MC, 3 CC) three times, (pick up and knit 1 CC, 1 MC) three times, pick up and knit 1 MC; place marker for start of instep stitches, work across instep stitches in pattern as per Houndstooth Chart row 1; place marker for end of instep stitches; along the second side of the heel flap (pick up and knit 1 MC, 1 CC) three times, pick up and knit 1 CC, (pick up and knit 1 MC, 3 CC) three times; place marker for new start of round.

82 (90, 98) stitches total. 36 (40, 44) on the instep, and 46 (50, 54) on the sole.

Gusset round 1:
On this round, you'll place two more markers for the gusset stitches. There are 5 gusset stitches each side, to be worked in a stripe pattern. The rest of the sock is worked in the Houndstooth pattern, starting with row 2. For size S, the round starts with st 4 of row 2 of the Houndstooth chart; or size M, the round starts with st 1 of row 2 of the Houndstooth chart.; for size L, the round starts with st 3 of row 2 of the Houndstooth chart.

Starting with st 4 (1, 3) of Houndstooth Chart row 2, work in pattern to 5 stitches before start of instep stitches, place marker B for gusset; (k1 MC, k1 CC) twice, k1 MC; work across instep stitches in pattern as per Houndstooth Chart row 2; (k1 MC, k1 CC) twice, k1 MC; place marker B for end of gusset; work to end of round in pattern, starting with st 1 (1, 1) of Houndstooth Chart row 2.

Gusset round 2: Starting with st 4 (1, 3) of Houndstooth Chart row 3, work in pattern to first gusset marker; k1 MC, k1 CC, k1 MC, k2tog MC; work across instep stitches in pattern as per Houndstooth Chart row 3; ssk MC, k1 MC, k1 CC, k1 MC to second gusset marker; work to end of round in pattern, starting with st 1 (1, 1) of Houndstooth Chart row 3.

Gusset round 3: Starting with st 4 (1, 3) of Houndstooth Chart row 4, work in pattern to first gusset marker; k1 MC, k1 CC, k2 MC; work across instep stitches in pattern, as per Houndstooth Chart row 4; k2 MC, k1 CC, k1 MC to second gusset marker; work to end of round in pattern, starting with st 1 (1, 1) of Houndstooth Chart row 4.

Gusset round 4: Starting with st 4 (1, 3) of Houndstooth Chart row 1, work in pattern to first gusset marker; k1 MC, k1 CC, k2tog MC; work across instep stitches in pattern, as per Houndstooth Chart row 1; ssk MC, k1 CC, k1 MC to second gusset marker; work to end of round in pattern, starting with st 1 (1, 1) of Houndstooth Chart row 1.

Gusset round 5: Work in pattern as established to first gusset marker; k1 MC, k1 CC, k1 MC; work across instep stitches in pattern as established; k1 MC, k1 CC, k1 MC to second gusset marker; work to end of round in pattern as established.

Gusset round 6: Work in pattern as established to first gusset marker; k1 MC, k2tog MC; work across instep stitches in pattern as established; ssk MC, k1 MC to second gusset marker; work to end of round in pattern as established.

Gusset round 7: Work in pattern as established to first gusset marker; k2 MC; work across instep stitches in pattern as established; k2 MC to second gusset marker; work to end of round in pattern as established.

Gusset round 8: Work in pattern as established to first gusset marker; k2tog MC; work across instep stitches in pattern as established; ssk MC to second gusset marker; work to end of round in pattern as established.

Gusset round 9: Work in pattern as established to first gusset marker; remove marker, k1 MC; work across instep stitches in pattern as established; k1 MC, remove second gusset marker; work to end of round in pattern as established.

Gusset round 10: Work in pattern as established to 2 stitches before instep, k2tog MC, work across instep stitches in pattern as established; ssk CC; work to end of round in pattern as established. Note: these final decreases are worked on the last gusset stitch and the adjacent stitch from the sole.

72 (80, 88) stitches total: 18, 20, 22 repeats of the Houndstooth chart.
Work even in pattern as established until foot measures 7 (8, 8.25) inches from back of heel, ending with chart row 4. You can adjust for a longer or shorter foot here, simply work until foot of sock measures 2 inches less than full length of foot from back of heel to toe. Remove start of round marker on the final round. Leave instep markers in position.

Setup for toe:
Setup round: (K1 MC, k1 CC) 3 (3, 4) times; place marker for new start of round; (k1 MC, k1 CC) to end of round (new position).

Decrease for toe:
Note: in the decrease, you will sometimes have two stitches in a row worked in the same color.
Work a decrease round: Work in vertical stripe pattern as established to 3 stitches before start of instep, (k2tog MC, k1 CC, k1 MC, ssk CC), work in vertical stripe pattern as established to 2 stitches before end of instep (k2tog MC, k1 CC, k1 MC, ssk CC), work in vertical stripe pattern as established to end of round.

Work 3 rounds even.
Work a decrease round followed by 2 even rounds, twice. (6 rounds total.)
Work a decrease round followed by 1 even round, three times. (6 rounds total)
Work decrease round 4 (6, 8) times, until 32 stitches rem. Work 8 sts in pattern to get to the end of the sole stitches.

Finishing:
To close up the toe, work a three-needle bind off as follows:
Cut yarns, leaving 12-inch tail of both. Slip sts to scrap yarn, and turn the sock inside out.
Slip 16 stitches of instep to one needle, and 16 stitches of sole to another. Line up the needles together, parallel.
Using MC, knit 1 st from front needle together with one from back. *Knit 1 stitch from front needle together with 1 from back; lift first stitch on right-hand needle over second stitch and off the needle, as for a standard bind off. Repeat from * until only 1 st rems. Pull MC tail through final stitch to secure.

Block and weave in all ends. The best and easiest way to block a sock is to get it wet, roll it in a towel to dry it a little, and then put it on. Remove it immediately and hang to dry.

WHAT'S NEXT

For more on color theory, particular as it applies to crafting, the best book you can buy is *Color Works: The Crafter's Guide to Color* by Deb Menz.

For general colorwork, Margaret Radcliffe's *The Essential Guide to Color Knitting Techniques* is an excellent reference book.

If you want to dig deep on Fair Isle specifically, go to the masters: *Alice Starmore's Book of Fair Isle Knitting*, and Sheila McGregor's book *Traditional Fair Isle Knitting*.

For specific patterns, look at Kaffe Fassett's *Kaffe Knits Again*, Kristin Nicholas's *Kristin Knits*, and Fiona Ellis's *Inspired Fair Isle Knits*.

MASTER GLOSSARY & LEGEND

alt	alternate; every other
C4L	Cable 4 left: slip the next 2 stitches to a cable needle and hold in front; k2, then k2 from cable needle; see Cables chapter
C4R	Cable 4 right: slip the next 2 stitches to a cable needle and hold in back; k2, then k2 from cable needle; see Cables chapter
C8R	Cable 8 right: slip the next 4 stitches to a cable needle and hold in back; k4, then k4 from cable needle; see Cables chapter
cm	centimeters
cn	cable needle
dpns	double-pointed needles
foll	following
gm	gram, grams
k	knit
k2tog	knit 2 stitches together
k3tog	knit 3 stitches together
kfb	knit front and back; see Shaping chapter
m	meter(s)
M1	make 1; see Shaping Chapter
M1L	make 1 left; see Shaping chapter
M1R	make 1 right; see Shaping chapter
M1Z	backwards loop make 1; see Shaping chapter
oz	ounce, ounces
p	purl
p2tog	purl 2 stitches together; see Shaping chapter
p3tog	purl 3 stitches together; see Shaping chapter
patt	pattern
pm	place marker
rem, rems	remain, remains
rep	repeat
rnd, rnds	round, rounds
RS	right side
s2kpo	slip the next 2 stitches together as if working a k2tog; knit the following stitch, and pass the 2 slipped stitches over it; see Shaping chapter
sk2po	slip the next stitch as if to knit; k2tog, then pass the slipped stitch over the k2tog; see Shaping chapter
skp	slip 1 st, knit the following stitch, and pass the slipped stitch over the knit stitch; see Shaping chapter

sl	slip a stitch: insert the right needle into the next stitch as if to purl, and slip it over to the right needle without working it; unless stated otherwise, always slip the stitch as if to purl
sl m	slip marker
ssk	slip the next 2 stitches, one-by-one, as if to knit; insert the tip of the left needle from left to right into the fronts of these two stitches; knit them together; see Shaping chapter
sssk	slip the next 3 stitches, one-by-one, as if to knit; insert the tip of the left needle from left to right into the fronts of these three stitches; knit them together; see Shaping chapter
st, sts	stitch, stitches
T3L	twist 3 left: slip next 2 stitches to cable needle and hold in front; p1, then k2 from cable needle
T3R	twist 3 right: slip next stitch to cable needle and hold in back; k2, then p1 from cable needle
tbl	through the back loop; see Socks Chapter
w&t	wrap and turn; see Socks chapter
WS	wrong side
yd, yds	yard, yards
yo	yarnover

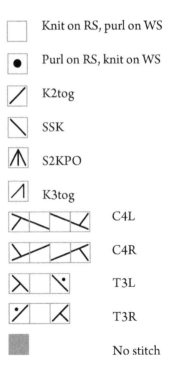

	Knit on RS, purl on WS
●	Purl on RS, knit on WS
╱	K2tog
╲	SSK
⋀	S2KPO
⫽	K3tog
	C4L
	C4R
	T3L
	T3R
	No stitch

BIBLIOGRAPHY

- **ALLEN, PAM**, *Lace Style*, Interweave Press, 2007, ISBN 978-1596680289

- **BORDHI, CAT**, *New Pathways for Sock Knitters, Book One*, Passing Paws Press, 2007, ISBN 978-0970886965; *Personal Footprints for Insouciant Sock Knitters*, Passing Paws Press, 2009, ISBN 978-0970886927.

- **BUDD, ANN**, *Getting Started Knitting Socks*, Interweave Press, 2007, ISBN, 978-1596680296.

- **BUSH, NANCY**, *Knitting Vintage Socks*, Interweave Press, 2005, ISBN, 978-1931499651; *Folk Socks*, Interweave Press, 2012, ISBN 978-1596684355; and *Knitting on the Road*, Interweave Press, 2001, ISBN 978-1883010911.

- **ELLIS, FIONA**, *Inspired Fair Isle Knits: 20 Creative Designs Inspired by the Elements*, Potter Craft, 2007, ISBN 0307346862

- **FASSETT, KAFFE**, *Kaffe Knits Again*, Potter Craft, 2007, ISBN 978-0307395382

- **GALESKAS, BEV**, *The Magic Loop - Knitting - Working Around On One Needle - Sarah Hauschka's Magical Unvention*, Fiber Trends, 2002, ASIN B000WWWZ54

- **HEMMONS HIATT, JUNE**, *Principles of Knitting*, Touchstone, 2011, ISBN 978-1416535171

- **JOHNSON, WENDY**, D. *Socks from the Toe Up: Essential Techniques and Patterns from Wendy Knits*, Potter Craft, 2009, ISBN 978-0307449443)

- **MENZ, DEB**, *Color Works: The Crafter's Guide to Color*, Interweave Press, 2004, ISBN 978-1931499477

- **MCGREGOR, SHEILA**, *Traditional Fair Isle Knitting*, Dover Publications, 2003, ISBN 978-0486431079

- **MICHELSON, CARMEN AND DAVIS, MARY-ANN**, *Knitter's Guide to Sweater Design*, Interweave Press, 1989, ISBN 0-934026-33-5

- **MODESITT, ANNIE**, *Confessions of a Knitting Heretic*, Modeknit Press, 2004, ISBN 978-0975421901

- **NICHOLAS, KRISTIN**, *Kristin Knits*, Storey Publishing, 2007, ISBN 978-1580176781

- **OBERLE, CHERYL**, *Folk Shawls*, Interweave Press, 2000, ISBN 978-1883010591

- **PARKES, CLARA**, *The Knitters Book of Socks*, Potter Craft, 2011, ISBN 978-0307586803

- **RADCLIFFE, MARGARET**, *The Essential Guide to Color Knitting Techniques*, Storey Publishing, 2008, ISBN 978-1603420402

- **SINGER, AMY R.**, *No Sheep for You*, Interweave Press, 2007, ISBN 978-1-59668-012-8

- **SOWERBY, JANE**, *Victorian Lace Today*, XRX Books, 2008, ISBN 978-1933064109

- **STANLEY, MONTSE**, *Knitter's Handbook: A Comprehensive Guide to the Principles and Techniques of Handknitting*, 1999, Reader's Digest Association, ISBN 978-0762102488

- **STARMORE, ALICE**, *Alice Starmore's Book of Fair Isle Knitting*, Dover Publications, 2009, ISBN 978-0486472188

- **SWANSEN, MEG**, *A Gathering of Lace*, XRX Books, 2005, ISBN 978-1893762244

- *The Vogue Knitting Stitchionary Volume Two: Cables: The Ultimate Stitch Dictionary from the Editors of Vogue Knitting Magazine*, 2006, ISBN 978-1931543897, Sixth & Spring Books

  The Vogue Knitting Stitchionary Volume Two: Cables: The Ultimate Stitch Dictionary from the Editors of Vogue Knitting Magazine, 2006, ISBN 978-1931543897, Sixth & Spring Books

  The Vogue Knitting Stitchionary Volume Five: Lace: The Ultimate Stitch Dictionary from the Editors of Vogue Knitting Magazine, 2010, ISBN 978-1933027937, Sixth & Spring Books

  Vogue Knitting: The Ultimate Knitting Book, Sixth & Spring Books, 2002, 978-1931543163

- **WALKER, BARBARA**, *A Treasury of Knitting Patterns*, Schoolhouse Press, 1988, ISBN 978-0942018165

  A Second Treasury of Knitting Patterns, Schoolhouse Press, 1998, ISBN 978-0942018172

  Charted Knitting Designs: A Third Treasury of Knitting Patterns, Schoolhouse Press, 1998, ISBN 978-0942018189

  A Fourth Treasury of Knitting Patterns, Schoolhouse Press, 2000, ISBN 978-0942018202

SUMMING UP...

The goal of this book is to help you take the next steps as a knitter—to make you more confident about choosing and working from patterns, and to encourage you to take on new types of projects like lace and colorwork.

Once you've built your skills you can progress to more challenging projects. Definitely seek out the books I've recommended, and search sites like www.knitty.com, www.patternfish.com and Ravelry.com for patterns.

If you love knitting socks, as I do, then there are so many great patterns, techniques, and constructions to try. And no matter what other sorts of knitting you enjoy, there are sock patterns to tempt you—cabled socks, lace socks, colorwork socks—even designs that combine techniques. Once you're feeling confident, try knitting two socks at the same time—usually worked on magic loop or two circulars.

If you enjoy cables, then the next step is garments. I adore classic Aran sweaters, and there are patterns for styles both modern and traditional. If an adult garment seems daunting, start with a kid's garment or a vest. My favorite cabled sweater of all time is Jenna Wilson's Rogue Hoodie, available from www.thegirlfromauntie.com.

If lace is your thing, I encourage you to explore the grand lace knitting traditions in Shetland, Estonia, and the Orenburg area of Russia; many books have been published focusing on these region's lace patterns. And lacework isn't just limited to scarves and shawls—there are thousands of patterns for garments using lace patterning.

If colorwork piques your interest, there are so many wonderful hat and mitten designs—they make very beautiful and very practical winter gear. And then from there, investigate classic Scandinavian designs like Dale of Norway's amazing ski sweaters, and the wide range of free patterns available from the Norwegian company DROPs, at www.garnstudio.com.

No matter what you enjoy, knit with confidence and a spirit of adventure!

ACKNOWLEDGMENTS

Many thanks are due to everyone who supported and help me throughout this process:

All my students over the years for teaching me how to teach, and for telling me what they need to know.

Shannon for taking a chance on me.

Megan Ingman, Denny MacMillan and the Lettuce Knit crew for so much encouragement and assistance. Jennifer Campbell and Miko Schechter and the rest of the gang at the Purple Purl for their help and support. And Lorena Klingel and Lisa Farmakovski of the dearly departed Naked Sheep for helping me get started.

My test knitters: Sarah Fay, Vanessa Iofolla, Lyndsey Isaac, Ashley Kearns, Robbie Laughlin, Brenna MacDonald, Kirsten Nelson, Vicky Norton, Jen Patola, Joycelyn Poon, Rochelle Ribeiro, Wendy Setterington, Bridgette Schirmer, Tammy Sutherland, and Lynn Wyminga.

The very generous yarn companies who supplied some of the gorgeous yarns: Diamond Yarns, Estelle Yarns, Kertzer, Louet Yarns, Schaefer Yarns, Sweet Georgia.

My readers: Andrea Addario, Tamara Krievins, and Lynne Sosnowksi.

Natalie Selles for the excellent tam pattern, and the author headshot.

My family for their endless love, support and encouragement, and Dexter, for testing out the cat toy, even though he's a dog.

ABOUT KATE ATHERLEY

attention to detail is everything

Kate was taught to knit as a child by her grandmother, Hilda Lowe. Hilda was a legendary knitter in her own right and Kate remembers with great fondness all the sweaters Hilda knitted for her. A family legend—sadly unconfirmed—says that Hilda used to earn a penny turning the heel of socks for knitters in her neighborhood, when she was a girl.

Kate, however, is a mathematician and refugee from the technology industry. She is known for her "small start" approach to teaching sock and mitten knitting.

Kate is Knitty's Lead Technical Editor. And she says it's just about her dream job. She is also the Knitting Editor for Canada's *A Needle Pulling Thread* Magazine and a regular contributor to books and magazines, including *KNIT* (formerly *Yarn Forward*) in the UK.

Kate regularly teaches at many stores around Ontario, including The Purple Purl and Lettuce Knit in Toronto and Shall We Knit in Waterloo. She's also a regular instructor at Toronto's Downtown Knit Collective events, and the Creativ Needlework Festival.

She lives in Toronto with her husband Norman and their rescued hound-dog Dexter. In her spare time, Kate likes to drink strong coffee and watch fictional detectives solve murder mysteries on television.

wisehildaknits.com

ABOUT COOPERATIVE PRESS
partners in publishing

Cooperative Press (formerly *anezka media*) was founded in 2007 by Shannon Okey, a voracious reader as well as writer and editor, who had been doing freelance acquisitions work, introducing authors with projects she believed in to editors at various publishers.

Although working with traditional publishers can be very rewarding, there are some books that fly under their radar. They're too avantgarde, or the marketing department doesn't know how to sell them, or they don't think they'll sell 50,000 copies in a year.

5,000 or 50,000. Does the book matter to that 5,000? Then it should be published.

In 2009, Cooperative Press changed its named to reflect the relationships we have developed with authors working on books. We work *together* to put out the best quality books we can and share in the proceeds accordingly.

Thank you for supporting independent publishers and authors.

cooperativepress.com

CPSIA information can be obtained at www.ICGtesting.com
Printed in the USA
BVOW07s1638300915

420341BV00006B/16/P